GREAT RESTAURANTS OF THE

HAMPTONS

THE EAST HAMPTON STAR

GREAT RESTAURANTS OF THE HAMPTONS

EATING WELL

ON THE SOUTH FORK

❋

Sheridan Sansegundo

Photos by Morgan McGivern

❋

NEW YORK   SAG HARBOR

HARBOR ELECTRONIC PUBLISHING
2004

WWW.HEPdigital.com

This book is dedicated to the many good-hearted friends who have accompanied me to restaurants over the years, enduring long drives in lousy weather for uncertain reward when they would much rather have been at home watching "The Sopranos."

❄ ❄ ❄

Printed in the United States of America

First printing: June 2004

CREDITS

Editor: Helen S. Rattray

Cover design: Dimitri Drjuchin

Cover photograph: "Jackson Pollock's Backyard," by Ken Robbins.

courtesy Lizan Tops Gallery, East Hampton NY

A NOTE ON THE TYPE

This edition is set in Adobe's release of Meridien. Designed in 1957 by Swiss typographer Adrian Frutiger for the French foundry Deberny & Peignot, Meridien's large x-height enhances legibility, while its Latinesque serifs and flared stems give it a classical Roman elegance. One of the pioneers of "cold type" design, Frutiger is perhaps best-known for the influential Univers family. The display type is Gill Sans. The type was set by UNET 2 Corporation.

CONTENTS

FOREWORD

Restaurant reviewing is a journalistic job that nearly everyone, including your brother-in-law and your Aunt Fanny, thinks they'd be darling at. The chance to sample all those meals and have someone else pay for them seems like a prize beyond pearls. It isn't. Think of all those impossibly inept dishes one must taste and try to assess fairly before a truly praiseworthy meal can be found to write about.

There's also the problem of trying to convey tactfully when food and service is sub-par and you live in a small town and all the restaurant owners and chefs have your photo pinned to the kitchen door with a dart. Not the same as knocking a terrible restaurant in a large national food magazine or daily newspaper where the offended can't get at you.

In times past, especially before food writing became more sophisticated, the restaurant "reviews" were just window dressing for the advertising department and of no real use to anyone, with comments like "tasty" and "big servings."

But the dining scene on the South Fork long ago became a venue for some fancy eateries and Culinary Institute of America-trained chefs, so The East Hampton Star, where all these reviews appeared originally, needed a food reporter with a discerning palate and a bright style of writing. No longer could the writer get away with reeling off the dishes available, their restaurant's nationality, and the prices.

Sheridan Sansegundo, who covers many other subjects for The Star, brings an easy conversational tone to her reviews with refreshing prose like "the zestless Caesar salad, although a very generous portion, was a prim maiden aunt in comparison to its salsa-dancing, thong-bikini-wearing sister (the baby beet, walnut, Bibb lettuce, and radicchio salad)."

Like any critic of anything, Sheridan brings to the job her particular tics, a love of soft-shell crabs, and her loathing of loud music obliterating conversation in many local restaurants. She called the crab at a Montauk restaurant the "ne plus ultra of soft shell crabs, a ticket-to-the-Super-Bowl crab, a triple-crown crab" in a burst of encomium.

Sheridan's reviews are careful and balanced and she tempers criticisms with whatever good points she can find about the places she goes. And she goes everywhere: from the chic of celebrity haunt Nick and Toni's, to the obscurity of a Chinda's, a little Thai joint buried on the Noyac Road. You get an entertaining assessment of the ambience, quality of the food and wine, and typical prices at the ever-changing restaurant scene on the East End.

So many restaurants spring up like mushrooms after a fall rain and then shrivel and die before a single year is out you have to get used to directions that include descriptions and names of the places that previously inhabited the premises: like "that's on Main Street in Sag Harbor where Phao used to be and before that a local bar and grill called Ryerson's across the street from the long-gone old saloon called Sal and Joe's."

Miriam Ungerer
Sag Harbor
April 2004

INTRODUCTION

For nearly 10 years I have been reviewing restaurants in the Hamptons, schlepping out to Montauk in a snowstorm, getting lost on Noyac Road, sitting in the ferry line on Shelter Island for hours, all in search of good food at fair prices.

Each spring a new crop of restaurants opens when the shadbush blooms, and each fall another crop succumbs to the Grim Dicer.

There seems to be an endless supply of investors wanting to be in the restaurant business in the Hamptons, but not necessarily an endless supply of talented chefs or reliable waitstaff, and after Labor Day there is no longer an endless supply of diners, either. Close for the season, and you lose your staff. Stay open, and you face empty tables the minute the weather turns foul.

Some meals I have eaten have been superlative, some so bad that I would have laughed if they hadn't been so expensive. There were dishes that stayed in the mind — a fierce Thai green curry, a saffroned fish soup that could have been served in Marseilles, a plate of blowfish — and others I wish I could forget — medallions of pork as hard as hockey pucks, chicken breasts like chunks of fiberboard, and endless fruit pies with soggy crusts and glutinous fillings. But very good or very bad can enliven a review.

What I began to dread over the years was opening a menu and finding the same things found everywhere — grilled salmon, rare crusted tuna, steak, roast chicken... (though described in much more pretentious language, of course). On the other hand, similarities gave my tablemates and me a chance to compare restaurants by the quality of their crab cakes, swordfish, and calamari.

As we are surrounded on the South Fork by the most wonderful fresh ingredients, it makes sense to concentrate a menu around them: fresh fish, clams from the bay, luscious tomatoes and strawberries in season, and the best sweet corn in the world. Also, when customers are unpredictable it makes sense to stick to fast, simple dishes. What is the point of spending hours over a cassoulet, a coq au vin, a bechamel sauce, if no one is going to order it?

But I must admit to a soft spot for those restaurants that go out on a limb with slow cooking or daring recipes. Too many follow the dish du jour like a flock of sheep. I would like to suggest a moratorium, for example, on crème brûlée, bread pudding, and flourless chocolate cake.

The reviews in this book cover about three years and most of the leading Hamptons restaurants. There are some omissions, usually because the review was out of date, but some older reviews have been included because they were still relevant. (Please note that my assessment of prices is relevant to the date of the review.)

The one thing we can all agree on is that the South Fork now offers such variety — Thai, Japanese, Colombian, Costa Rican, Mexican, Pacific rim, French bistro, Cajun, and the best of American — that everyone can find a favorite. And if we feel we are being Hamptoned, that is, overcharged for dull food served by waiters with attitude, then we can vote with our feet.

Sheridan Sansegundo
East Hampton NY
May 2004

ABOUT THE AUTHOR

Sheridan Sansegundo was born in England, home of mysterious meat pies and overboiled vegetables. She became seriously interested in cooking and eating after spending time in France and then settling in Spain for ten years. She came to East Hampton in 1980 and is The East Hampton Star's arts editor. She has been reviewing and writing about the Hamptons restaurant scene for nine years.

GREAT RESTAURANTS OF THE HAMPTONS

ABOUT THE WEBSITE

Great Restaurants of the Hamptons includes carefully selected reviews of what we consider the most interesting kitchens in the area. But there are many more places to eat in the Hamptons. Moreover, restaurants change all the time. Owners move on, chefs and entrees come and go with the seasons or even in between. Yesterday's hot spot may be boarded up tomorrow. Conversely, by the time you read this, some new and interesting places will have debuted. Such is the nature of the restaurant business.

For these reasons we created HamptonDining.com, a comprehensive website where the most up-to-date information about your favorite East End restaurants can be found.

An integral running commentary on the book, HamptonDining.com includes:

- Capsule reviews of more than 200 restaurants and take-out joints from Westhampton to Montauk
- Features to help you select where to dine (kid-friendly, waterfront, etc.)
- Links to the restaurants' websites, latest reviews, special offers, and restaurant news.
- Online menus, and more.

We invite you to log on.

See you at dinner!

Amagansett &
Napeague

CLAM BAR

Montauk Highway on Napeague
Amagansett
267-6348
Lunch and dinner daily. Seasonal. No Reservations. No credit cards.

There is one thing that makes me feel that summer is really here. It is not swimming or warm nights or barbecues on the beach, it is the first time that I eat at one of the South Fork's casual outdoor cafes. It could be any one of a dozen, most of which are east of Amagansett, but the Clam Bar is a perfect representative.

There are tables with umbrellas, lots of small children, T-shirts, flip-flops, and mellow Caribbean music. The place is run with military precision by Special Ops waitresses in tank tops, shorts, big smiles, and lots of sunblock.

Clams are the big attraction, of course, and good value at $11 a dozen. They certainly couldn't be fresher, and they make the perfect start to your summer getaway meal. (Not that it is a quiet, rural getaway, since there are big, black sport utility vehicles zooming past in an unbroken stream, like a swarm of mosquitoes in the tundra.)

There's a big list of daily specials, which on Sunday included swordfish, lobster chowder, steamers, and tuna bits, and the regular menu with its staples of mussels ($9.50), hamburger ($4), lobster roll ($11), crab cakes ($6.50), lobster (a one-pounder was $9 last week) and fried everything — clams, shrimp, oysters, scallops, fish and chips, and chicken nuggets.

But I'm going to jump ahead to the best menu addition I've seen this summer. Because half the world seems to be on the Atkins diet, and also because, let's face it, when you order a lobster roll it is not the roll that gets you excited, the Clam Bar is serving a big helping of perfect lobster salad on half a big, sweet, deseeded, drained tomato, cut open like a flower. It is as good a way of spending $15 as I can think of right now.

If you have a chance, do try the Cajun popcorn shrimp ($6.50), which have a spicy, peppery bread coating and somehow go with the place — summery and fun. The tuna bits ($7.50) were

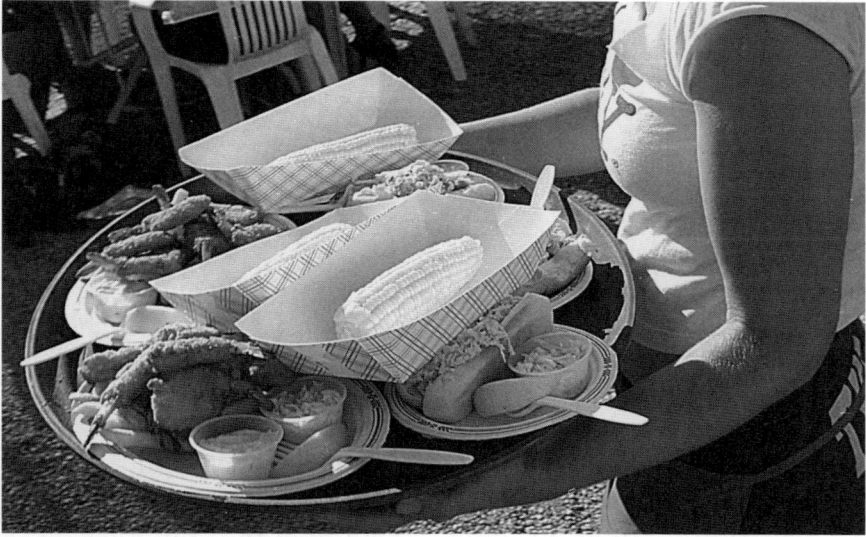

not such a success. They were deep-fried in a heavy batter, and overcooked. I seem to remember they used to do tuna bits with no batter that were much better. Or perhaps they oughta boughta better batter.

The crab cakes are not made with that very special A-list, black-tie crab, but were still very good, even if they were B-list, Bermuda-shorts crabs.

The steamers ($14.50) were lovely — just think of all those Atkins dieters who can now slosh them in the melted butter without feeling any guilt. It was very hard to decide which was better, the lobster salad on tomato or a simply extraordinary piece of swordfish ($12.50) that made me think that all those swordfish slices I have tasted over the years must have been from some poor relation.

And what could be better, after having stuffed yourself with seafood, than to sit back with iced coffee and a slice of a great Key lime pie and play "first one to spot a fuel-economy car wins $10."

It is not a bad idea when you have eaten to hang a left on Napeague Harbor Road and work off the meal in the Walking Dunes. You can see all the way to Connecticut and there's not a sound except the breeze. Summer is here.

July 2003

ESTIA CANTINA

177 Main Street
Amagansett
267-6320
Breakfast, lunch, dinner, and late night bar menu daily.

Estia in Amagansett has changed its name to Estia Cantina, but regulars need not worry, there will still be spinach and feta cheese omelets and blueberry pancakes for breakfast and homemade pastas for dinner.

The name change reflects an increasing number of Mexican dishes on the menu, but mainly signals that from 10 p.m. to midnight Estia will be open for tortillas, tamales, Latin music, and a tequila tasting menu.

The restaurant business on the South Fork is not for wimps. First of all you have a frenziedly busy summer balanced by a pretty dead winter and then you have competition, lots of competition.

Some owners find their particular niche and stick to it, others, like Colin Ambrose of Estia, are constantly trying something new. Every winter for the past 10 years he has gone away to study different cuisines or the work of different chefs and the results show up on the menu, at least at dinnertime.

If you live east of Southampton, then it is a good bet that some time over the years you have had lunch at Estia, which started life one step up from a diner and still retains the look, even though the menu is a very different animal now. It boasts many ardent regulars, partly because any place in the Hamptons where you can drop in at 8 a.m. for a plate of eggs, home fries, bacon or sausage, O.J., and coffee for $7 is a gem beyond compare.

Although I had heard good reports about it, last week was the first time I had been there for dinner. Two bits of information rang very loud bells — Estia has its own kitchen garden and Estia makes its own pasta.

I am one of those people who, given a choice, would as soon order pasta in a restaurant as shredded wheat for dessert. But since this is what Estia is known for we ordered two, both very simple, one with a tomato sauce with olives and feta cheese ($15)

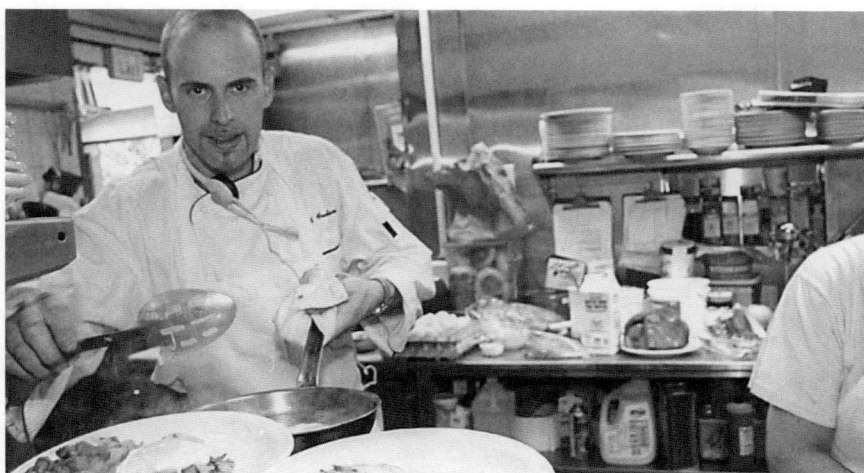

and the other with tomato, basil, garlic, and red wine ($14). Everything I had heard is true — they really are exceptionally good.

The other entree we tried was a special of the day that was also included in the $19.95 midweek prix fixe: soft-shelled crabs that were so good they would have undoubtedly thought the sacrifice worth it had anyone asked them.

For appetizers, it is a hard choice between the chicken and roasted corn quesadilla ($7), which we chose and which was excellent, and crabmeat tostadas or three different tamales — roasted corn and pineapple, chicken and avocado, and shrimp in cilantro cream.

We also tried two different salads, both of which were rather disappointing. The roasted beet and goat cheese salad turned out to be 90 percent mixed greens, as was the chopped salad, which just had a few bits of corn, onion, and cucumber bouncing around in it. They were both $8, no bargain.

An exceptionally good espresso finished the meal, with rather soggy profiteroles filled with first rate ice cream and a very nice blueberry crumble.

Wines by the glass, at about $7, included a so-so merlot and a lively Spanish red. The bread is not only supremely good but arrives with a little heap of herbed white bean paste and olive oil. Nothing wrong with the service either.

Estia is a chameleon: a friendly, eggs-any-style diner for breakfast; a bustling sandwich and salad lunch spot; quiet and cozy with a sophisticated menu for dinner, and a lively bar scene, catching much Talkhouse overflow, after 10 p.m. But any way you look at it, it is now as much a part of the warp and weft of Amagansett as the Farmers Market or Vinnie the barber.

May 2002

GORDON'S

231 Main Street

Amagansett

267-3010

Open for dinner nightly except Mondays.

Glancing at a 1997 review of Gordon's in Amagansett, I see that I remarked on the restaurant's remaining unchanged since I first ate there in the early 1980s. Well, guess what: It's *still* exactly the same.

On the other hand, outside this Brigadoon of a restaurant everything else is changing too fast. Familiar vistas sprout dot-com mansions over-night, relentlessly trendy eating places open with glossy magazine coverage but flit at the end of the season, and there's no down time in the winter any more.

So a restaurant that remains frozen in time — that sticks to its guns and serves vegetables in separate little dishes and where the chef and the maitre d' and the menu have hardly changed in a quarter-century — starts to look like an old friend.

The focus of the decor here is a handsome cut glass chandelier that hangs rather incongruously from an acoustic tile ceiling. That's not a criticism — after a recent dining experience that was extremely painful decibel-wise, acoustic tile is one of my favorite expressions. Gordon's also has carpeting and so conversation is a pleasure instead of an impossibility.

Gordon's has an excellent wine list, hot bread arrives promptly, and the service is conscientious and attentive, if some-what leisurely.

From Sunday through Thursday the restaurant offers a $24 prix fixe meal consisting of an appetizer, entree, and coffee, and since the selection is wide this would seem to be the way to go.

On the other hand, the à la carte prices won't bankrupt you either: appetizers start at $4.25 for a mixed green salad with smoked salmon at $9.75 being the ceiling and entrees are from $15.50 to $26.75 for a veal chop, the only item over $25.

That mixed green salad is a bargain as prices go these days, being large, extremely fresh and varied, and with an exemplary

vinaigrette. At $4.75, a tart, invigorating arugula salad is also a good choice.

An appetizer-sized portion of cannelloni — once on every menu in the Western Hemisphere, still on Gordon's — was as rich and comforting as it was when you loved it as a child but not nearly as heavy as it usually is. But if you are wavering between the two I'd say definitely choose the big, plump, wine-stewed mussels. They're such fun to eat, too.

There are 4,400 species of crabs, all of them edible, and those that hie from Maryland must be high on the list, as opposed to, say, the 12-foot Japanese giant crab, which must present rather a problem in the kitchen.

At Gordon's, a plate of rice arrives first and the steaming crab meat in its wine and herb broth is dashed to the table and ladled out at the last minute. Try it — this is a wonderful dish.

Of the perfectly cooked, crisp-outside, pink-inside salmon there is not much to be said except that it was a much bigger piece than you get elsewhere, which means I will be enjoying what's left of it this evening.

Gordon's is known for its fish dishes, but don't allow this to deter you from trying the sirloin steak. One member of our party would not be dissuaded — steak was what she wanted and steak was what she was going to have — and when it came it was beyond belief good.

In addition to the very good creamed spinach we all received, she got a nice baked potato, which was better than the rather dull rice.

The Long Island duck, which came with an apricot brandy sauce and bouncy wild rice, was very good, if somewhat over-shadowed by the other entrees.

Desserts include such favorites from the past as peach Melba and coupe aux marrons. We tried another old warhorse, crème caramel, which is always a good way to end a meal, and a chocolate mousse that was a pudding rather than a mousse but tasted none the worse for that.

As I said at the beginning, Gordon's hasn't changed. This also means that the quality of the food, reliably good, hasn't changed, either, nor have the prices changed much — which makes Gordon's very good value for the money.

March 2002

THE LOBSTER ROLL

Montauk Highway on Napeague

Amagansett

267-3740

Lunch and dinner six days. Closed Tuesdays. Seasonal.

Restaurants come and restaurants go, but Lunch, as the Lobster Roll is called because of the large sign on its roof, goes on forever.

It is open only in the summer — how else could it be when the place personifies flip-flops and sandy children eating French fries?

Everyone knows the place is child-friendly, but, with the Napeague stretch becoming more like the Indy 500 every day, it is worth mentioning that Lunch's outdoor patio (equipped with crayons on the tables) is fenced in and completely safe for toddlers. It is adult friendly, too, with charming waitstaff and super-rapid service.

Having got that out of the way, I have only one word to say. Puffers.

There was a time that you could go out in a rowboat off the East End and haul in puffers, or blowfish, by the dozens. For some reason they seem to have disappeared from around here, but after a long search the Lobster Roll has found another source. They are served fried (as is much of the menu), and they are wonderful. Sometimes called chicken of the sea, they are like small boneless chicken legs, but with a more delicate flavor.

The menu has changed little over the years. You'll always find chowders and mussels and onion rings and fried calamari and Lunch's famous lobster roll. But these days you will also find plenty of charbroiled fish dishes and fish and vegetable burgers.

Appetizers start at $3.50 for a small green salad or $4.50 for chowder and rise to $9.95 for mussels or $13.95 for a puffer appetizer. After that, there's everything from a $6.50 fried clam-strip roll to soft shell crabs at $18.95. There is a selection of beer on tap and wines by the glass and there is an excellent children's menu.

Lunch offers what might be called homemade fast food, its kitchen being organized in an assembly line manner, with mussels

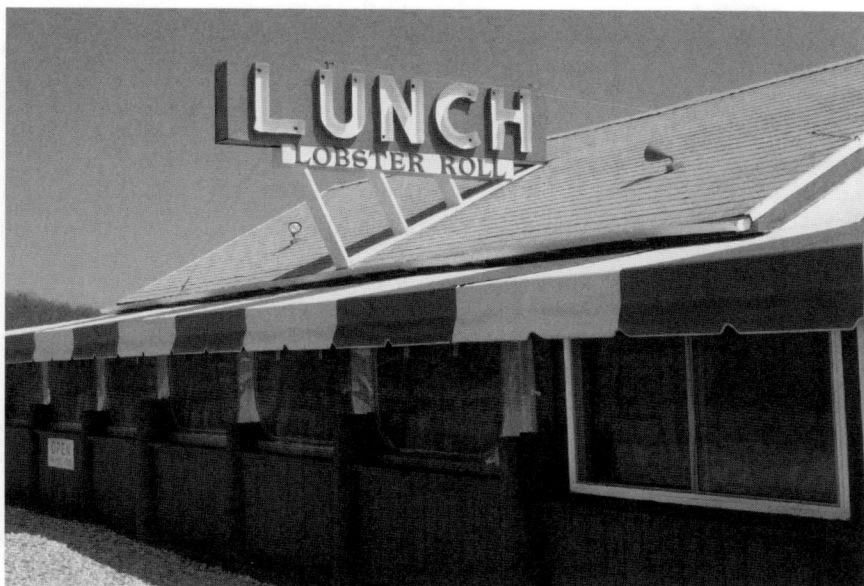

and steamers encased in net bags for easy cooking. This can have its drawbacks — there is not much room for finesse.

Our steamers were rather bland and flabby, for example, as were the pan-seared scallops, a not very generous portion for $17.50.

Another thing that hasn't changed over the years are the blah crinkle-cut French fries. With practically everywhere on the South Fork now serving good, fresh fries, these are due for an upgrade.

The fresh fish platters, on the other hand, are completely up to date, with both the tuna and swordfish, which are served with salad or fries, getting high marks. They come with a particularly good coleslaw. And, although the one we tried had rather a lot of celery on this occasion, you can't go wrong with the lobster roll. The soft shell crabs are also highly recommended.

When it comes to dessert, the Lobster Roll's pies are always a sure bet.

Lunch is Lunch, an East End institution, and long may it continue. It is not particularly cheap considering the nuts and bolts setting, and the menu is heavy on the deep-frying, but what it does well, it does very well.

June 2002

MOUNT FUJI

27 Montauk Highway
Amagansett
267-7600
(Also at 1670 North Highway, Southampton)
Open seven days for lunch and dinner.

In the years since Mount Fuji in Amagansett gave itself a make-over and became pretty and friendly, with excellent food at reasonable prices, it has become a local favorite.

The restaurant, whose décor is clean and stylish with lots of blond wood, is always busy, but they can usually fit you in somewhere. It is divided into two sections, a large dining room with a choice of tables or traditional Japanese booths with low tables and a smaller room that has tables, a bar, and a sushi bar.

The bar scene is popular. The customers are perhaps attracted by the wild specialty drinks, some of which, believe me, you would rather not know about.

Although sushi and sashimi are the main attraction, the menu is huge and undoubtedly has something for every taste — tempura, 16 different types of teriyaki, marinated octopus, big bowls of noodles with shrimp tempura or fish cakes, tuna or striped bass in ginger sauce, deep-fried sea bass among them.

Most people seem to find a few favorites and then order them again and again. The pretty lacquered Bento boxes, which are served with soup and salad, are very popular. For $22.95, for example, you get five pieces of sushi, a California roll, beef negi-maki, shumai (dumplings), and Japanese pickles. The sushi deluxe, 10 pieces and a tuna roll, is $18.95.

And then there are the chef's special rolls, no fewer than 37 of them. It is one of Mount Fuji's more endearing features that they appear to be named after regular customers, so that alongside such dishes as unajyu, tonkatsu, and sunomono, you have the Eddie roll, the Melony roll, the Potter roll, the Donna roll, the Ralph roll, and the Gavin roll.

Two particular favorites of our reviewing crew are the Miller roll ($11.95), spicy yellowtail with scallions topped with tuna and avocado, and the Amber roll ($10.95), which is a divine combina-

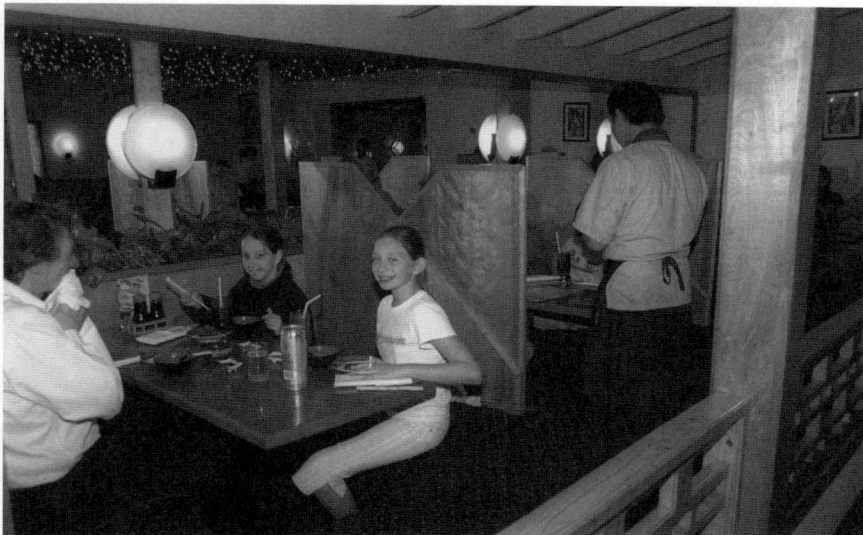

tion of spicy tuna, avocado, smoked crab meat, and crunchy fried fish.

But on this occasion we vowed to order only new dishes from the special menu, which meant that we discovered some new and intriguing things that we might not otherwise have tried.

We tried the Tom roll ($12.95), which in texture resembled the Amber roll — I would be hard pressed to say which I thought better — but with shrimp tempura and caviar topped with spicy tuna. I think that both were edged out, however, by the spicy lobster roll ($10.95). Beautifully presented, the lobster meat was combined with scallions and cucumber with the rice on the outside rolled in caviar.

For $5.95 you get a plateful of a dozen tiny deep-fried crabs. A couple of crunches and they're gone, but they are fun while they last.

Salmon skin salad — somehow it doesn't sound likely to make its way onto the best-seller list, as in, "I'd sell my mother for a bowl of salmon skin salad right now." But the salad, a mixture of crisp salmon skin, eel sauce, and flying fish roe served over that nice green seaweed, is actually quite delicious.

A little more conventional, and perhaps a good choice for those readers who just went "Yuck!" at the thought of salmon skin salad, is the fluke katsu, a generous plateful of breaded fluke with a slightly spicy mayonnaise ($7.95).

Choosing a dessert is always a bit of a minefield at a Japanese restaurant. You are always safe at Mount Fuji to choose the fried banana, which is wonderful, or green tea ice cream. But this time we consulted the menu to see if there was anything unusual.

"Are my eyes deceiving me or does that say 'deep-fried cheesecake'?" said one of our party in disbelief. What could we do? We had to try it.

And we guiltily agreed that, although this particular serving was spoiled by still being frozen in the center, it was rather nice. I'm not sure that I would recommend it as a dessert, except to sugar-deprived 10-year-olds, but it certainly tasted better than it sounds.

If you are around at lunchtime, then the Maki lunch special is recommended — soup, salad, and a choice of two rolls for $7.95.

Mount Fuji is a comfortable and comforting place to go. Equally a place where you can duck in in your work boots on a cold night for a steaming miso soup and a beer or come with a bunch of friends to sit Japanese-style and eat from elegant lacquer and stoneware.

January 2004

NAPEAGUE STRETCH
Route 27
Amagansett
267-6980

Some reviews are easy to write, particularly when there is an exciting new restaurant; others are hard: "Well, the bread was very good, and the steak was okay, and the view out of the window as we waited half an hour for the check was charming...."

And then, very occasionally, you come across a restaurant that you don't want to tell anyone about. Where the members of your reviewing team start threatening before the meal is over, "Don't review it now. Wait until September. Let's keep it a secret."

But fair is fair, and anyway, word of mouth is already spreading the news. Napeague Stretch, in a little building on the left as you drive to Montauk that has housed a different restaurant every season, has not only excellent food, charming decor, and delightful service, but prices that will take you back in time.

Without altering its basic structure that much, the building has been renovated into a light and attractive space with pine tables, comfortable director's chairs, and good lighting. Simple and summery. Anticipating the good weather that will surely arrive one day, there is now an outdoor dining area and a huge, well-designed bar (you get to look at other people instead of staring at your own face in a mirror on the other side of the bar).

As I have watched prices slowly drift upward while everyone's income stayed much the same, I had about given up on bargains. "It's the Hamptons," we'd say as the $10 green salad turned out to be the same as any other green salad. "What can you do?"

Well, the Stretch's green salad costs $4, its grilled chicken club sandwich with rosemary mayonnaise and fries costs $5 and was reported to us by a friend as being "the best bargain on the South Fork," shrimp in a basket with fries, $11. Caesar salad is $5, and a really good baby spinach salad with grilled mushrooms and onions and blue cheese, large enough to be shared, is $6.

The soup of the day was shrimp gumbo, which was very good, though it could maybe have been a little spicier. The large crab cake with red pepper aioli would have made an entree. It was

full of crabmeat, though a little ho-hum. The slices of rare tuna, on the other hand, were great, and came with an interesting fine-chopped salad of crabmeat, asparagus, artichoke, red onion, and fresh tomato.

The Oyster Po' Boy Sandwich is great value at $8, a big ciabatta roll (God bless whoever started bringing good rolls to the East End and freed us from buying those eight dead things in a plastic bag) lined with lettuce and thin, thin slices of tomato, stuffed with wonderful spicy cornmeal-crusted oysters. Plus fries. Plus slaw. Plus a good chili-pepper mayo.

The big, radiantly fresh tuna steak was excellent, with an interesting accompaniment of roasted potato slices and marinated vegetables. For sheer value, I think I have to vote for the fried chicken: three large pieces that looked as if they were going to be dry but were just the opposite, served with gravy on the side and the most wonderful roughly mashed, skins and all, potatoes: $10.

A special of the day was soft-shell crabs with thyme lemon sauce. There is nothing more delicious when it is cooked well than a soft-shell crab, and nothing worse if it isn't (it suddenly stops looking like seafood and becomes something from a B horror movie). These were terrific.

Another friend ("Don't review it! Please!") who went to the Stretch twice last week, reports that the fish and chips were wonderful — very light, crispy batter — and so was her huge bowl of penne in tomato basil sauce with artichokes and fresh mozzarella.

There is a small selection of desserts, not, we believe, made on the premises, including an impeccable New York cheesecake with a particularly nice crust and a good Key lime pie.

So there you have it — good food, pretty setting, outdoor dining, charming waitstaff, and great prices. Just leave a small table outside by the flowers for me, okay?

June 2003

PACIFIC EAST

415 Main Street
Amagansett
267-7770
Open daily for dinner. Bar open until 4 a.m.

Since my last visit to Pacific East in Amagansett they've added a sushi bar, which will come as good news to all those sushi lovers out there who believe there can never be too many.

We started our meal with a sushi selection and opinion was unanimous in its praise. We also liked the sound of the special rolls, among them one of lobster, caviar, and shiso and another of tempura prawn, asparagus, and creamy ponzu (a sauce made with seaweed, dried bonito flakes, lemon, sake, and such).

Just under $20 will get you a satisfying and lively selection of sushi; add a glass of wine and you will have had an enjoyable and reasonably priced meal.

Otherwise, one must say that Pacific East is one of the more expensive places around. Apart from a miso soup with vegetables at $6, appetizers run from $9 for an arugula and tomato salad to $19 for foie gras with a caramelized pear.

Vegetarian and noodle dishes are $15 or $16, otherwise entrees start at $23 for salmon to $42 for lobster. Rack of lamb is $36, Chilean sea bass is $28, roast chicken, $24.

But everything is so interesting, and, while the flavors are unusual, Pacific East does not put too many together at once, or ones that are discordant. How about a lobster and shiitake pancake with champagne kim-chi (fermented vegetable paste) or a tempura soft-shell crab with wasabi mustard guacamole?

The other appetizer we tried was a miso-rubbed chicken salad with spinach, sugar snaps, and wontons, a description that gives no idea of this delectable dish of matchstick-thin slivers of meat and vegetables, with contrasting textures and a marvelous flavor. At $10 it was a generous portion and an absolute treat.

When the sushi bar was put in, a dividing wall was removed from the dining room, so that now it is one big open space. The lighting is subtly atmospheric (so much so that you could hardly read the menu) and the open second story with its palm trees,

floating white draperies, and ceiling fans looks like a set for a Somerset Maugham drama set in 1940s Singapore. Very appropriate.

The wine list is not terribly large, but it includes a little of everything and ranges in price from stratospheric down to a good selection of inexpensive wines. Local wines are not neglected, including that nice Channing Daughters Fresh Red.

Roasted Japanese black cod, served over a delicious celery root and parsnip puree, was voted the winner among the entrees. For $29, the portion of fish was rather small but it was a dream, a masterpiece of a fish that had the whole table making good-food noises. The loser was the not-very-exciting noodles with shredded Peking duck and crisp vegetables.

The other duck dish, however, thinly sliced ovals of duck breast coated in pepper and served with stuffed pancakes and a rich, vinous huckleberry sauce ($26), was satisfying in all respects, and with just enough flavor surprises to add excitement.

The grilled mahi mahi was very spicy but not very inspiring and the Chilean sea bass, while nice enough, didn't seem $28 nice. We should probably have ordered the whole ginger-stuffed tempura red snapper with a hot dipping sauce — that sounds great.

But back to another winner — yellowfin tuna rolls served rare but quickly fried, tempura-style, and served with wakame seaweed and toasted sesame rice. Once again, it was the interesting combination of flavors and the careful preparation that made it a winner.

And talking of winners, every dessert we tried was outstanding. It's hard to say which was better, the baked Alaska with its eye-opening flavors of honey and lemon or the warm and comforting banana bread pudding, with its undertone of ginger and its dark rum sauce.

But we awarded the prize to a small chocolate pudding with a liquid center, served with white chocolate ice cream in a little wafer basket. It was incorrectly called a bomb instead of a bombe, but "bomb" was maybe a better description of that explosion of chocolate taste.

Our waiter was boisterously enthusiastic and helpful, but there were rather too many long waits. And I must express one quibbling peeve in the hope that someone might heed it.

However well meaning, it's irritating to have a waiter ask, evidently expecting a reply, "And how is everyone tonight?" Presumably if someone was not all right they'd be home in bed and not spending an arm and a leg in his restaurant.

But, held hostage by one platitude, one is obliged to reply with another to avoid a stalemate. "We're fine," seven middle-aged adults dutifully and inanely replied in unison.

When Pacific East opened, it was sublime. The combination of the delicate food, unusual flavors, beautiful presentation, and charming dinnerware made it seem worth every penny.

It's still very, very good — the cod and the chocolate pudding were as sublime as anything I've tasted in a long while — but it didn't seem to have quite the old magic on this occasion.

June 2002

Bridgehampton, Wainscott & Water Mill

ALISON

95 School Street

Bridgehampton

537-7100

Summer hours: Dinner six days. Closed Monday. Lunch Wednesday–Sunday.
Winter hours: dinner Thursday through Sunday. Brunch Saturday and Sunday.

Although it has nothing to do with food, I can't resist starting this review with a nice tale about Alison by the Beach, which was in a little old building with the sloping floors on the corner of Town Line Road and Montauk Highway in Sagaponack before it moved to Bridgehampton.

Ask the man in the street what picture comes to mind with the words "Alison by the Beach" and the answer would probably be something like "chi-chi food for summer people." But when the Fairway restaurant at the Poxabogue Golf Center across the highway, everyone's favorite bacon and eggs joint, was closed down, it was Alison who stepped up to the plate and invited Fairway's owner to share the premises. Fairway served breakfast and lunch and Alison served dinner as usual.

Some bureaucratic tick soon put an end to that, of course, but for a while there it was a delightful example of neighbors being neighbors.

Alison has been on the South Fork for a while now, and has built up a faithful clientele for its simple but elegant menu, which changes seasonally, its simple but classy decor, and its friendly service.

On a recent night, we found appetizers expensive — $8 for a green salad or lentil soup or $11 for a romaine lettuce salad with pine nuts, for example. Entrees, on the other hand, were not so bad, all under $25 except for lamb shank at $27 and a sirloin steak at $34.

On Thursday and Sunday evenings, and for early birds before 7 on Friday and Saturday, there is a two-course prix fixe for $19.95 or three courses for $26. Weekend brunch is served on the patio when weather permits.

The impressive wine list is predominantly French and predominantly expensive. But there is a decent selection of those that are cheaper or American.

The service was as friendly as ever, though there were a few glitches such as the arrival of bass in place of halibut and a cute busboy, obviously new, who cleared away all the silverware just as our entrees were about to arrive.

Although it is a little pricey at $12, the warm scallop salad was an outstanding appetizer. An orange and tarragon vinaigrette gave the scallops a sweet and sour kick, and I just loved the salad of finely shaved fennel, with its summery Mediterranean tang of aniseed.

Equally good was a very simple salad of yellow and red beets with goat cheese, frisée, and pistachios. The generous portion of green salad had a very carefully balanced dressing but at $8 did seem a little steep.

We asked about striped bass being on the menu, knowing that it was out of season, and gave good marks to the restaurant for coming straight out and admitting it was from a fish farm. When it was brought to the table mistakenly, it looked so good that the guest who had ordered halibut almost decided to settle for it.

But he didn't, which was good because the halibut turned out to be exemplary, gently steamed to the exact second and served with braised artichokes and white asparagus. It was the sort of simple dish that looks as if any fool could do it, until any fool tries.

The second excellent entree of the evening was roast chicken. There's no better test of a restaurant than seeing what it will do to that culinary albatross, the chicken breast. It is usually some sort of a cop out involving sauce, but Alison's was not gussied up in any way, just extremely tender, extremely flavorful chicken.

The sirloin steak, served with bordelaise sauce and some fabulous shoestring potatoes, was large and cooked exactly as had been requested. Not much more to say about it than that, however. The lamb shank was enjoyable and very tender but needed to have been simmered with something with a little more punch, something that would have infused the meat with its flavors a bit more. As it was, it tasted muttony. It was accompanied by a rather discouraged selection of beans.

While the lamb fell off the bone with tenderness, that, alas, could not be said about the daily special, neat disks of loin of pork so tough they could have been used as hockey pucks.

Desserts include a delicious warm Valrhona chocolate soufflé cake, which East End chefs all seem to make. This was a fine example though. We also tried a nostalgic root-beer float and, by far and away the winner, a cardamom and mocha-flavored crème brûlée with a beautiful, subtle flavor. The temperature and the caramelized coating were just right.

April 2003

ALMOND

Montauk Highway
Bridgehampton
537-8885
Dinner six days. Closed Wednesday.

Almond, an inexpensive French bistro-style restaurant, has opened in the spot that used to be the Woodshed, on the Montauk Highway just west of Bridgehampton Commons. It is bigger than it was, with a back deck glassed in to make an airy dining room, and prettier, with lots of window boxes and planters.

We were there on a Sunday night and, although the restaurant had only been open a couple of weeks, it was nearly full and there were a bunch of people drinking at the bar.

To start the meal you could choose a classic leek and potato soup for $6, short ribs and onions served hot or cold for $9, or splurge on a $14 foie gras mousse. There is a good selection of salads, from a mixed green salad at $7 through a hearty Niçoise for $12, and inexpensive entree items such as a hamburger or a Croque Monsieur.

If you don't see what you want among the appetizers, you might want to look at the list of side dishes, all $5, which include macaroni and cheese, white bean and duck confit gratin, ratatouille, and cod brandade, as well as more conventional choices.

The wine list is French, though there are a couple of South Fork wines, with about 60 percent of the bottles under $30. The wines by the glass — a good Wölffer Estate chardonnay, an excellent cabernet sauvignon, an okay merlot, and a rather nasty pinot noir — were $5 or $6.

We were served by one of Almond's owners (the other is the chef), a man of large personality who does much to contribute to the friendly, laid-back atmosphere of the place. He asked us about the wines, agreed about the pinot noir, and brought us a round of a lovely Chateauneuf du Pape on the house.

Having got off on the right foot with good bread and first rate butter and olive oil, and intrigued by that unusual list of side dishes, we ordered the cod brandade for an appetizer. There was a

good deal more mashed potatoes than cod in the dish, but who cared, it was delicious. It was served with two slices of crisp, garlicky fried bread.

You get a big plateful of good fat mussels, for $7 but the winning appetizer was definitely the rillettes (meat or fish cooked slowly in seasoned fat and then pounded to a rough paste) on sourdough croutons, two of salmon and two of duck.

The one miss was the snails, which sounded exciting because they were cooked with garlic and Pernod. Unfortunately, far too much Pernod had been used. It was frustrating, because you could tell they would have been delicious.

On the inexpensive end of our entree choices there was the most delicious pressed roast pork sandwich ($9) and, on the expensive end ($19), a big portion of sliced rare steak with French fries. The steak was served with a rich reduction with chives and roasted onions and topped by a delicious chunk of marrow. A fine dish of baked striped bass in a pleasant garlic and saffron sauce came with carefully cooked haricots verts.

The leg of lamb with white beans and ratatouille was not as good. A roast leg of lamb, served thinly sliced and pink, is a prize beyond rubies; it's also beyond the capabilities of most small restaurants. Pre-cooked leg of lamb just doesn't cut it — better stick to lamb chops or a rich lamb stew of some kind.

For dessert we tried a tarte Tatin and, what else, almond ice cream.

Almond has only just opened and there are a couple of wrinkles still to be ironed out, but it's a comfortable space, the service couldn't be nicer, the menu is imaginative, and heaven knows the price is right.

May 2001

BOBBY VAN'S

2393 Main Street
Bridgehampton
537-0590
Lunch and dinner seven days.

If you drive past Bobby Van's in the summer, when its full-length windows are folded back and the place takes on the air of a sidewalk cafe in Paris, it always seems to be full. It always seems to be full at night, too.

If you decide to visit for yourself to see what the fuss is about, you will soon find out — the place has a lovely atmosphere.

When the venerable hangout of writers like James Jones and Irwin Shaw was sold in the 1990s, it was given a face-lift that transformed it from a cozy, smoke-impregnated cave to something light and airy and smart — but new, without history or patina.

It has acquired that over the intervening years, and now you have a restaurant that is attractive and gemütlich, with lazily turning ceiling fans, warm lighting, and just the right amount of wood. The tables are well spaced and the sound level is fine, despite the busy adjoining bar.

In the bar, chalkboards announce the daily specials and two silent televisions flicker with "Close Encounters" oblivion.

There is a sensible range of wines by the glass and a wine list that offers plenty of reasonable choices. Service is fast and efficient and unobtrusive, with maybe one "How is everything?" too many the night we were there.

Appetizers are $10 to $14. Entrees vary widely — you can have a burger for $10.50, a number of inexpensive entrees, some regular entrees from $20 to $26, or one of the restaurant's specialty steaks from $32 to $36.

The menu offers interesting choices. Appetizers include the usual crab cakes, mussels, Caesar salad, and Clams Casino, but also a Thai shrimp taco and a smoked salmon, goat cheese, and pine nut Napoleon. There's your roast chicken and your sesame-crusted tuna but also a curried shrimp and quinoa salad.

If you are there any night but Saturday in the off-season, however, go for the $25 prix fixe. The winning meal of the

evening, we decided, was the one chosen from that menu — a wonderful ginger and carrot soup followed by a hefty, blackened ribeye steak with excellent mashed potatoes. A pleasant Apple Brown Betty brought up the rear.

The rest of our orders were a bit more hit-or-miss. A salad of Bibb lettuce with baby yellow beets, walnuts, and radicchio was great, but the zestless Caesar, although a very generous portion, was a prim maiden aunt in comparison to its salsa-dancing, thong-bikini-wearing sister.

Bobby Van's does a terrific carpaccio of filet mignon, a beautifully presented plateful dressed with baby arugula and shaved reggiano that was a delight.

Although it arrived more well done than had been requested, the restaurant does a fine, fat hamburger. And in the comfort food department, there is an amazing shepherd's pie the size of a small shepherd's hut, for $18.

I think the only real disappointment of the meal was a daily special of almond-crusted sole. It was somewhat dry and dull and didn't seem to have any almonds. When this was mentioned to the waiter, he went to check with the chef and told us that the fish was, in fact, dipped in finely crushed almonds.

Our complaint had been only a mild one, but when we received the bill we found that we had not been charged for the dish. Now that was above and beyond the call of duty.

At Bobby Van's you can sit at the bar and have some bar food, you can order inexpensively or push the boat out with oysters and a porterhouse steak, or you can grab the excellent prix fixe. But what will bring you back to the place is its comfortable, charming atmosphere.

November 2002

MIRKO'S

Water Mill Square

Water Mill

726-4444

Dinner six days. Closed Monday. Winter hours: dinner Thursday through Sunday.

Mirko's is only hard to find the first time. Once you have negotiated the winding parking lots and darkened storefronts that constitute Water Mill Square at night, you'll find it again. Just ignore those companions trailing behind you and saying, "It can't be back here."

On a winter night, the little restaurant casts a warm light on brick walkways like something out of a Currier & Ives print; in the summer, there's a tranquil outdoor dining patio. Inside, there's a small bar area with a European feel and a single dining room which is comfortable and relaxingly simple.

Mirko's attracts a very sleek crowd: pulled-back hair with pearl studs, wingtips and suits, and restrained voices — not that the latter would matter one way or another, because the restaurant has excellent acoustics and no music.

The service must be mentioned because it is on an unobtrusive and totally professional level that is seldom encountered on the East End, land of the amiable college-break waiter who bounces in saying, "Hi, I'm Greg."

You want to pick your wines carefully. As the wines by the glass are $7 or $7.50 each, it pays to buy a bottle if your table mates can agree on it. But the wine list needs a little negotiating, as it is liberally peppered with $80, $100, and $150 land mines. We chose a Gigondas '96, a light southern Rhone red that was agreeable to everyone and cost $32.

The bread that was served, though hot and perfectly adequate, did not match the excellent herb butter that was provided.

The menu prices may make you flinch a little, with appetizers from $8.25 for a green salad to a number of $12.95 items and entrees starting at $19.95 for rigatoni Bolognese and climbing to $31.95 for a grilled veal chop.

Some of those appetizers are very substantial, however, particularly the Croatian stuffed cabbage, which is the one item on the menu that hints that the chef is Croatian. It's a big helping of a simple plain dish but it's feather light, if one can say that of stuffed cabbage.

The last time I dined here, the crab cakes were one of the standouts; this time they were the only disappointment. It wasn't that they were unpleasant, just heavy and somewhat viscous.

I recommend the delicious little cholesterol nuggets made up of fat shrimp in straightjackets of bacon with a lemon, shallot, and white wine sauce. They were very popular, to the extent that the reviewer had to pull rank to get any at all, but they paled beside the calamari.

Eating this highly developed invertebrate in other places, as I have noted, can be like eating the rubber bands that imprison lobster claws.

Disillusioned, I almost didn't try them on this occasion. But I'm glad that I overcame my reluctance because at Mirko's, served naked and tender in a lemon, garlic, and sherry wine sauce, they were superlative.

It wasn't the winning appetizer, however. That spot was reserved for a Napoleon of portobello mushrooms, secured to a heap of wild rice and pecans by a rich compote of tomatoes and shallots. It was a veritable circus act of lively flavors and textures.

Among the entrees that we didn't try, but which were very good on an earlier occasion, were braised short ribs and roast duck. We did try the horseradish crusted codfish ($26.50), which could have done with more horseradish but which was served with perfect mashed potatoes and topped with an amusing frizz of deep-fried shredded leeks.

The pan-roasted salmon ($26.50) was beautifully cooked and was served with vegetables that made a perfect complement: roast fennel and a notable Swiss chard.

Particularly recommended is the pork tenderloin, a generous portion of a most unporkly tenderness flavored with sage which was served with a delicate apple compote and a hearty sweet and sour mixture of shallots.

To end our meal, we tried a nice little pecan pudding and a dessert whose basis was caramelized oranges. Both were fine, although not memorable.

Mirko's is a serious professional restaurant run by a husband and wife team, the husband cooking, the wife running the front of the house with great geniality. It's definitely expensive, but it's very good.

Perhaps you should do as we did: Choose a bottle of wine carefully and share appetizers and desserts, or pick a second appetizer instead of an entree. Sauteed spinach with oil and garlic, a side dish, would make a good starter at $6. It's quite possible to stay within a budget with a bit of imagination.

For instance, I was the fortunate one who chose the portobello mushrooms ($11.95) and I followed it with another appetizer, the calamari ($10.59), which was more than enough. It was a just-about-perfect meal, and it cost in total less than most of the entrees on the menu.

Of course, if you're feeling flush, you don't have to hold back. Go ahead, pig out.

March 2000

PIERRE'S

2468 Main Street

Bridgehampton

537-5110

Dinner seven days in season, Until midnight Friday and Saturday.
Lunch on weekends.

So I was driving along Montauk Highway on the way to eat at Pierre's in Bridgehampton last Thursday in a state of the deepest weltschmerz, or at least with a lack of enthusiasm, headed for a restaurant spot that I seem to review every five minutes — Boom Bistro, the Bull's Head, the Independent, Lure, who knows what else, all of them mainly famous for a late-night bar scene.

But if I went in through the door as the Grinch, I left as a smiley face button.

The wine list did not do much to dispel my prejudice, having only two reds and one white under $30 and wines by the glass being mainly $9 to $15. Nor did the menu strike me as very exciting, having all the old Hamptons dining warhorses such as grilled salmon, calamari, lobster, chicken, and filet mignon.

But once we got to the food....

The place itself is visually charming, pale green and white with soft lighting and a strikingly elegant bar. Right on Bridgehampton's Main Street, the side windows look out onto the lawn and garden of the Hampton Library. There was music, but it was good French music, and moreover our waitress lowered the volume when we asked.

My mood started to change as I heard a chatter of French from the kitchen and realized that behind Pierre's there really is a Frenchman: Pierre Weber, whose family has been in the food business for five generations. And when we got a plate of tostadas with a fine white bean and parsley dip. And when I found on the table a pot of fleur du sel, the finest sea salt, which retails at the Hamptons Ripoffery for two arms and a leg.

And then there was a midweek prix fixe for $20, surely one of the best bargains around at this time of year. (I am told that

another great bargain at Pierre's is the $5 lobster salad panini served at lunch on Fridays and Saturdays.)

Otherwise, appetizers are $8 to $16, salads are $9 to $16, and entrees are $18 (penne with tomatoes) to $28 (filet mignon).

A plain green salad was enlivened by a pungent aniseed bite, maybe from fennel, while an immaculate tomato and mozzarella salad was served, blessedly, at room temperature. The salmon tartare ($14) had its own surprise, little crunchy cubes of jicama and an avocado dressing.

The winning appetizer was voted the tomato terrine, which was a delicate tomato, basil, and garlic aspic studded with big chunks of lobster. And the ceviche was no slouch — one fat lime-soaked shrimp balanced on the edge of a glass of pungent marinated seafood that positively raised the hairs on the back of my neck.

From start to finish, the presentation was pretty enough to bring tears to the eyes.

When we moved on to the entrees, the good news continued. For one thing the chef has an amazing way with potatoes, be they French fries, whole roasted baby potatoes in their skins, or the best gratin Dauphinois I've tasted in years.

Right up there at the top of the could-not-have-been-better list was a piece of cod that had been roasted so that it was crisp and brown yet barely cooked through in the center. It was served on a mound of sauteed vegetables and the two were melded with a lemon and white wine sauce with a touch of cream. Lovely.

The filet mignon came with those excellent fries, jailbait haricot verts, and a pepper sauce. It was excellent, but the cheaper hanger steak, with its macho charred flavor and red wine sauce, packed more of a punch.

Linguini with cockles, Little Necks, and razor clams was a nice dish, with the cockles providing an extra zest (but we couldn't find any razor clams). And then there was the ultimate restaurant test, the Begum of Boring: roast chicken breast. Pierre's passed with flying colors. It had flavor, it had moisture, one would have ordered it again.

And Pierre's doesn't fall down on the desserts. Unfortunately the banana Tatin with dulce de leche parfait was sold out, because that sounds great. However, the hot melting chocolate cake, a Hamptons cliché if ever there was one, was superb, as was the raspberry Napoleon filled with a silky panna cotta.

We also noticed that Pierre's has a lively bar menu, offering bruschettas, tartines, French fries with a garlic dip, and other appetizing little snacks ranging in price from $8 to $14 (lobster bruschetta).

The menu at Pierre's may not look so exciting, but the secret is all in the preparation — what arrives on your plate will take you by surprise. The prices are fairly expensive but there are bargains to be had, service is fine, and the ambience is relaxed, with a definite European touch.

August 2002

ROBERT'S

755 Montauk Highway
Water Mill
726-7171

Dinner seven days, July and August Otherwise dinner six days. Closed Tuesday.

Another summer has leaked away, leaving the East End with a small mountain of lobster carapaces, clamshells, and corn shuckings to show for it. And, it is hoped, some favorable gastronomic memories.

But you never know; people are always grabbing my elbow and griping that they have just spent the price of a Mercedes convertible for a mediocre meal somewhere. So, for this last weekend of the season, I wanted a surefire winner so I could write a cheery review and summer could go out with the food critic's equivalent of the best olive oil.

I picked Robert's in Water Mill with a little trepidation. When it first opened in the spring of 1999 it qualified as my pick of the year, but I was concerned that it would be one of those horses that come out of the starting gate too fast. Would it still be up there with the leaders or would it have dropped to the back of the field?

I need not have worried: From the grilled fresh sardines to the best fruit pie I can remember eating, the meal we had was memorable, the kind you are still thinking about when you wake up the following morning.

Robert's is in a substantial, square colonial house a few doors from the white-steepled community center on Montauk Highway. The place has been charmingly converted, with lots of open beams and old wood. There is a limited amount of outdoor dining on a brick patio with nifty heaters for chilly nights, a small bar, and two interconnecting dining rooms. The farther one is preferable. Because of its low ceilings, when the place is full (and judging by the elaborate reservation system it is usually so) it is very noisy, our only criticism of the evening.

Prices are consistent with those you would find at any of the 40 or so posher restaurants on the East End, with all entrees over $20 but under $30 (except for Black Angus steak, $34, crab cakes,

$31, and the occasional daily special). But at Robert's you really get your money's worth, which is by no means always the case.

Appetizers are a little higher than usual, $10 to $16, but Robert's gives major play to its contorni, side dishes, which means that as an appetizer you can also choose from among six wonderful vegetable dishes, at $7 to $11. And while Robert's does everything well, the restaurant's touch with vegetables deserves particular mention.

The cuisine is based on that of Liguria, the Italian Riviera, that narrow strip of coastal plain backed by mountains known for its fishing ports, salami, pesto, and chestnut trees. An exceptional rough peasant bread is brought to the table wrapped in a cloth in Ligurian style.

Service is brisk and efficient; the wine list leans toward Italy but has plenty of choice and a good selection of reasonable bottles. The $28 Geografico Chianti pleased everyone (though the dry martinis could have been drier).

Even though tempted by such appetizers as fennel and red onion salad with local peaches or prosciutto with figs, three of our party chose straightforward vegetable dishes: escarole with garlic, broccoli rabe, and roasted beets with fresh mint and shredded onion. Believe me, with vegetables like these you could give up meat and never miss it.

The beets, in particular, were as good as any beet could hope to be. This wonderful vegetable, the favorite of Emperor Charlemagne, is often underappreciated or, as in England, where they pickle it in vinegar, downright mistreated.

We also tried the two special appetizers of the day. One was fresh sardines, filleted, given a dusting of coarse breadcrumbs, grilled, and then reconstituted into a fishy shape and served. Too good!

The other was panzanella, an Italian bread salad made with onions, peppers, tomatoes, basil, balsamic vinegar, and olive oil. The bread squares, which in this case had a wonderful silken texture, are usually soaked in iced water and squeezed dry before being added to chopped salad and left to infuse the flavors for several hours.

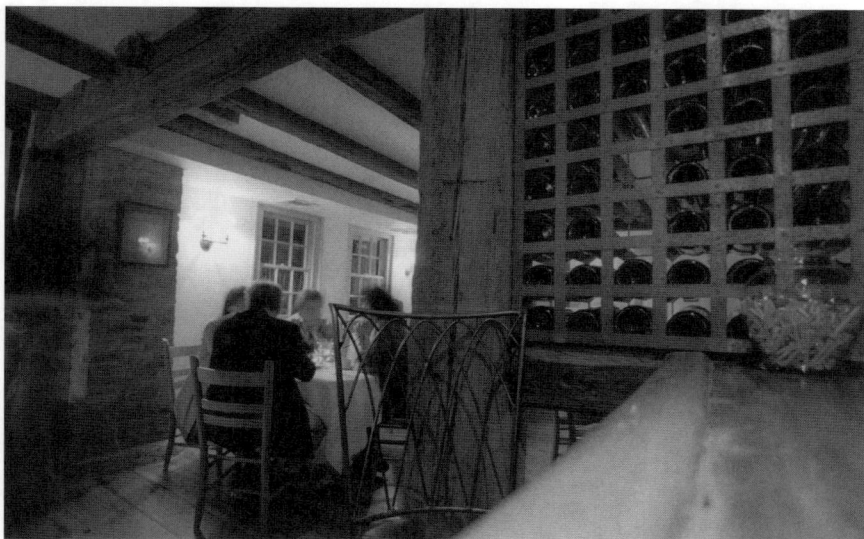

I make a panzanella myself of which I am very proud, but my self-esteem suffered a severe blow after trying Robert's. Let's just say it was like tasting Roquefort after a Kraft cheese slice.

Then it was on to the *secondi piatti,* which included a dish of tagliatelle with black truffles and Parmesan that was the ideal mixture of simplicity and subtlety: pasta as delicate cloud instead of pasta as big bowl of leaden starch.

A large piece of nicely cooked striped bass was transformed by its accompaniment of fresh morels on a bed of fava beans and roasted fresh corn. And the crab cakes were outstanding: crisply fried, they fell to pieces when touched by a fork, revealing the finest white crabmeat, no filler at all. They were almost overshadowed by the lemony shaved fennel salad that accompanied them.

One of the entree specials was veal saltimbocca, a Roman specialty of thinly sliced sauteed veal with sage and prosciutto, that was served on a bed of lightly cooked baby spinach. Anywhere else it would have been memorable; here it was rather put in the shade by the other dishes, particularly the other daily special, a spectacular Dover sole served on the bone.

If the appetizers are great, and the entrees are great, then you're not normally going to escape with the desserts also being great.

But Robert's managed to end its fireworks display with a fire-cracker finale. The almond cake with raspberry sauce brought tears to my eyes, but the peach and blueberry pie... that fruit and flavor-laden filling... that crisp, sugary, frangible crust... it was a pastry cook's three-handkerchief magnum opus.

Okay. I'm all raved out.

August 2001

SARACEN

Montauk Highway
Wainscott
537-6255
Dinner seven nights until late.

The old house on the creek at Georgica Pond in Wainscott, home to one culinary failure after another until Sapore di Mare made it a Hamptons hot spot, has a new tenant.

Saracen's owners have plenty of experience in the restaurant business, which would seem to be a necessity in managing the charming rabbit warren of lounges, porches, and dining rooms that ramble on different levels through the building.

It's a problematical space, but when it works, it's great. Our first reaction on a recent evening, however, was one of near panic as we were led to a table in a room where the noise of the music could only be described as horrific. Please, we begged, can't we sit somewhere else?

Without a moment's hesitation, the staff hurried to clear a table on the porch for us. That reduced the noise by half but there was a speaker right over our heads, so we had to complain again. This time they not only turned the music down, they also prepared another table in a room with no speakers in case we still weren't happy.

In short, they fell over backward to accommodate us, and the same kind of professional care and attention continued through the evening — complimentary *amuses-gueules,* baskets of excellent bread replenished before they were empty, and no attitude from anyone.

Which is not to say that Saracen, which has only been open a couple of weeks, has ironed out all the kinks yet — there was a very long wait for our appetizers — but you get the impression that the enthusiastic staff will soon have it mastered.

The Italian menu, with its emphasis on seafood, is imaginative without being bizarre. The prices are reasonable. I'll repeat that, in case you missed it the first time: *The prices are reasonable.*

Appetizers, most of which are rather special, are $7 to $11. Generous portions of pasta are $14 to $16 or a little more for lobster pappardelle. Entrees are $19 to $24, except for a 20-ounce porterhouse steak at $26.

There is also a daily risotto, which, since it varies from day to day, I suspect may be one of the chef's specialties.

The wide and well-chosen range of wines by the glass, between $7 and $9, are served in big glasses with portions to match. The arrival of our waiter with a tray of these bumper servings caused a brief respectful hush at the table.

The ethos behind the entrees seems to be fresh and not too fancy. The appetizers are more imaginative, offering, among other dishes I regretted not sampling, stuffed zucchini flowers, a marinated seafood salad, a grilled vegetable Napoleon, and baby artichokes stuffed with goat cheese.

But there was no way I wasn't going to try the *polpo scottato*, grilled octopus with a red wine sauce, which is every bit as good as it sounds. It even came with a tiny pyramid of mashed potatoes.

Tuna carpaccio, a large plate covered with lime-zested slices of raw tuna as thin as rose petals, was lovely, as were the grilled figs with gorgonzola and prosciutto, which brought Tuscan summer to the table.

Two guests shared a portion of linguini with fresh artichokes for an appetizer. Light and full of subtle natural flavor, it was somewhat preferred over the orecchiette with broccoli rabe and white beans, but it was a close call because the broccoli rabe was blissful.

If you have a hearty appetite, then go for the grilled porterhouse steak, which came nicely rare with a peppery sauce, but it is a dauntingly large slab of meat.

Seafood is where the restaurant shines. The Chilean sea bass was exactly the dish you dream of being served in a restaurant — perfectly cooked with those little extras like frizzled leeks that you wouldn't attempt at home.

High marks also to the swordfish and the tuna when it came back, having been returned for a bit more cooking (it was requested rare but came cold in the middle the first time).

Desserts were slightly less successful, though the ubiquitous chocolate mousse cake is of a high quality here. A blueberry crumble was interesting and pleasant, but the apple pie was a failure.

By the time we dragged ourselves away from the table, the restaurant was nearly empty, a sure sign that we had been enjoying ourselves.

High prices and not having any Manolo Blahnik mules have kept the ordinary diner away from this spot on the edge of Georgica Pond for many, many years, particularly in its last unlamented incarnation when all the entrees were over $30.

So, come back to the five and dime, Jimmy Dean, because Saracen is friendly, accommodating, elegant, and reasonably priced. One suggestion — if you are noise-phobic, request a table in one of the quiet rooms when you make your reservation.

August 2002

STAR ROOM

378 Montauk Highway

Wainscott

537-3332

Dinner Thursday through Monday. Tapas at 11:30 AM.

The first thing I feel obliged to say about the Star Room, the glamorous transformation of the Wainscott Annex restaurant, is that there were as many men and women eating there Sunday as men and men. It would be a shame to miss Kevin Penner's extraordinary green-curried scallops because you fear that you will be welcomed only if you are gay.

The second is that this is not another paean to reasonably priced new Hamptons restaurants. This one is expensive. And the portions are not very large. And the wine list will make you go "eek!"

But, oh, the food is good. Good enough that you will still be thinking about it the next day. Good enough to go back, high prices or not.

But first, the physical transformation. The old Annex had an unattractive entry and was rather dark (though it hadn't been the picture of Bohemian funk the Style section of The Sunday Times described for a very long time). Now it's white and airy, with slate-topped bars and an elegant spiral staircase that leads to an intimate upper-level dining room.

Floor-to-ceiling doors slide open to a charming patio with light-covered trees à la Tavern on the Green and amusing butter-yellow plastic furniture. The dining room has the most comfortable chairs you'll find anywhere and tables that drop pneumatically to cocktail lounge height for the late-night party scene. (Our table, it must be said, wobbled rather alarmingly.)

That's when the party crowd moves back and forth from the dance floor to the lounge or hangs out on the patio, high-powered DJs spin the vinyl, and the noise level increases.

There were five of us dining on Sunday. We were comfortable, we could carry on a conversation without shouting, and there was great music for the dinner-at-8 crowd — Chet Baker vocals, early Billie....

The service is fast, and the waitstaff, mainly young women, are extremely attentive if still a little green. That wine list? Wines by the glass are $8 to $16 and there are only three bottles under $30, none of them red. But it is an interesting and wide-ranging list, and the very nice Julienas Beaujolais they have at $33 won't break the bank.

The menu is small and stimulating, with choices for both the adventurous and the conservative, and the chef's hand is first felt in some interesting semolina bread rolls with raisins and fennel.

Appetizers start at $10 for a spicy coconut milk soup with shiitake mushrooms, cilantro, kaffir lime, and lemongrass and rise to $21 for foie gras with a special chutney. Most are $13 to $15. Entrees are $26 to $34.

Potato and mascarpone ravioli with brown butter and black truffles sound blandly heavy. Don't you believe it — they were delicate, subtle, delicious. On the other end of the taste scale were the langostinos with spicy green papaya (only two of the little fellas, unfortunately) whose marinade of lime, dried shrimp, peanuts, palm sugar, and chilies was like clashing cymbals and a trumpet voluntary.

On the quieter side, there was a nice salad of red and yellow beets with goat cheese and those adolescent salad greens that have swept through America like the dreaded kudzu.

The dish of the evening was decidedly those scallops, the chef's signature dish. There was the heat of chillies, a touch of ginger, a hint of some herb — terrific.

Two of the more conservative dishes were an extremely moist and tender chicken with both green and white asparagus and a thyme and lemon sauce, and a halibut, unfortunately a little overcooked but rescued by a lovely mushroom and truffle oil sauce and perfect potato puree.

But then it was back to excitement with the perfectly cooked lobster saffron risotto with Peekytoe crab, and a roast loin of lamb.

The lamb, a less than daunting serving, one must say, had the most wonderful flavor and was served with an eye-opening accompaniment of tomato and black olive confit over a mound of rosemary-flavored eggplant puree; complex flavors, but not too many of them.

All the desserts are $9. We didn't want to wait for the signature warm chocolate and peanut butter cake, which is cooked to order, so we tried a milk chocolate and caramel financier and a steamed lemon pudding with a passion fruit sorbet.

After what had gone before, I found them a little disappointing. The financier was pleasant, the sorbet was underwhelming, and the lemon pudding rather blah.

The owners have made clear that they want to attract a general clientele to the Star Room, and with a star chef and star prices they really need to, especially for the quieter evening hours before the club scene kicks in.

With so many restaurants to visit, it's seldom that I think about returning to the one I have just reviewed. But this time, I thought about the dishes I didn't try — the spicy coconut milk soup, the braised fresh pork belly (doesn't sound good, but there must be a secret), and the curried pigeon — and vowed I would have to go back. It's a real winner.

June 2001

SUKI ZUKI

688 Main Street
Water Mill
726-4600
Dinner six days. Closed Monday. Lunch Tuesday through Thursday..

If you want to stop griping for 10 seconds about the Hamptons building boom and think about the good things it has brought, high on your list (probably the only item on your list, come to think about it) would have to be the arrival of so many good restaurants.

One of the most recent is Suki Zuki, an elegant sushi and robata (Japanese open fire grill) gaff on Main Street in Water Mill that has taken over from one of those impenetrably gloomy fake Irish pubs whose menu was heart disease heaven.

There is an area of tables just inside the door and another at the back. Behind the long wooden counter there are two sushi chefs at one end and a robata chef, juggling skewers over leaping flames while listening to a Walkman, at the other. The decor is spare and subtle, with pretty frosted-glass, twig-covered lamps. The service was just a little distracted.

Prices are good. The sushi deluxe — one tuna roll, one California roll, and 10 different sushi pieces — is $25; appetizers are mainly $5 or $6, entrees are $15 to $20 and include miso soup.

Gyozo, steamed vegetable dumplings ($6), come to the table in an attractive cane steamer. They were made with greenish dumpling dough, had a delicate and distinctive filling, and were served with a fierce sauce. The fried pork dumplings were almost as good.

I had arrived chilled to the bone and in need of hot soup. When the miso kenchin, a miso soup with Eastern vegetables, came to the table it was the size of Lake Erie, a huge bowlful that could have been a full meal. Even though my companions, given spoons, also dipped in, we still didn't finish all of it.

We tried some particularly good pan-fried Long Island oysters, though we'd also been tempted to try sake-steamed mussels or Long Island blowfish. Suki Zuki, by the way, will offer you a

choice from among nearly a dozen different sakes and a good selection of wines by the glass.

I just love a good bargain. I was already purring about that giant $6 bowl of soup when I received my moriawase plate. This $8 robata sampler contained four skewers. One had little pieces of tender chicken, another had shrimp, another scallops wrapped in bacon, and the last had mini hamburgers. Apart from the latter, which were rather dull, they were all excellent.

That makes a filling and delicious meal for $14. Not bad.

Meanwhile my companions, sushi and sashimi freaks one and all, were ordering sea urchin and flying fish roe and eel and yellowtail as if they hadn't eaten for a week. Even so, the bill remained reasonable.

The sushi was exemplary. Beautifully served; beautifully fresh, with top honors going to a particularly delicious sea urchin and a spicy tuna roll. The same with the sashimi — even the mackerel, which is not a favorite of mine unless it was alive and biting a few minutes before, was good.

Wait, I'm not done yet. Ignore the rather bland ice creams and ask for a tempura banana. You'll thank me.

All in all, Suki Zuki is a very welcome addition to the East End restaurant scene.

April 2001

WORLD PIE

2404 Main Street
Bridgehampton
537-7999
Lunch and dinner seven days until midnight. Saturday and Sunday brunch.

When World Pie opened in 1999 I categorized it as an upscale pizza joint. Well, bite my tongue! This weekend we had a meal there that was as good, varied, and imaginative as any I have had on the South Fork in months.

In spite of the bitter cold weather, there were many diners and a throng of I've-gotta-get-outta-the-house-even-if-I-get-frost-bite merrymakers at the bar.

World Pie's main room, with its glossy redwood bar and plump banquette table in the window, is most attractive. The back room, which opens up to the outdoors in summer, is made cozier in winter by lighting so dim we couldn't read the menu.

Wines by the glass are $6 to $9 with a few, listed as "kick-ass wines," at $9 to $12. I advise ordering by the bottle, because the prices are very fair. A Marques de Riscal Reserve from Spain, for example, is well priced at $35. That is listed under "Hot Stuff." Other wines are listed under similarly cutesy headings such as "Crisp and Clean and No Caffeine," "Oaks and Apples," "Smooth," and "Bold and Beautiful."

There is a big menu with about a dozen each of appetizers, salads, entrees, and pastas, with the whole middle section devoted to over 20 different pizzas. As if that weren't enough, the list of specials on Saturday included four appetizers and six entrees.

World Pie is a restaurant for all pockets. Two people can have a beer, share a $12 pizza, and scarcely eat for less at home, or they can eat their way through the menu and spend a lot more.

If Crispy Artichoke ($9) is on the list of specials when you go to World Pie, grab it. This is the über-artichoke, artichoke multiplied by five, artichoke accorded beatification by the pope. We couldn't tell exactly how it had been cooked to make each petal crunchy but not tough, its center as sweet as honey, before it was crowned with green goddess dressing, but, then again, neither did we care.

From the regular menu came a reliable favorite, seared rare tuna slices ($10). The tuna was sparkling fresh and its lovely ocean flavor was perked up by its swim in some sort of spicy marinade beforehand. Served over sesame noodles and wakame seaweed it makes a great light starter.

Another winner was the grilled octopus salad ($9). The miniature octopi, pulled untimely from the sea, had a marvelous smoky flavor and the salad of pea shoots in a spicy lemon dressing with mixed olives was terrific.

After that, the shaved fennel and grapefruit salad ($8), though it sounded exciting with its crumbled asiago cheese, toasted pine nuts, and apple cider vinaigrette, was rather tame. Perfectly nice, mind you, but lacking the pizazz of the other dishes.

Having done well on the appetizers, World Pie did even better on the entrees. The one pizza we tried — sundried tomato, mozzarella, artichoke hearts, goat cheese, and roast garlic ($13) — was delicious and almost as good heated up the next day. Unlike with most pizzas, the crust stayed crisp. I mention this because I defy anyone to eat one of the small pizzas by themselves, so if you order one you'll have to persuade your dinner companions to help you out or take it home. It is too good to waste.

From the daily specials, we chose sautéed monkfish ($21), a fish of lovely texture but not a lot of taste. This one, served with lump crabmeat, lemon grass risotto, and kefir lime sauce, was totally successful and is highly recommended.

As is the tandoori chicken ($17). The chicken breast was very juicy and tender and rolled in tandoori spices and there was couscous served in a curry sauce, baba ganoush (a Mideast eggplant puree), and warm hummus. It provided a really interesting combination of flavors.

The lobster ravioli ($17), served with slow-roasted tomatoes, were very nice but the flavor of the lobster was not very apparent.

There is a fairly conventional list of desserts, including a homemade tartufo ice cream that was quite big enough to feed all four of us.

World Pie's motto is "Enjoy Life, Eat Out, and Play Bocce." I don't think there is going to be much bocce playing in the next

month or two, but if you eat out at World Pie, I think you will find that the first part of the motto will certainly follow.

January 2004

YAMA-Q

Main Street
Bridgehampton
537-0225
Open daily noon to 4 p.m. and 6 to 9:30 p.m., 10 on Fridays and Saturdays.

The first time I had Yama-Q's agadashi tofu it was under duress.

"A clear soup with lumps of tofu in it? No thanks."

It sounded impossibly dull. But my friend insisted, and eventually I gave in. Since then, returning many times to this minuscule restaurant on Bridgehampton's Main Street, I always look for it on the menu.

The lumps of tofu are deep fried, with a crunchy golden crust, and the scallion-laced broth is aromatic and pungently flavored. It would raise Lazarus from the dead.

Yama-Q, in the building that used to house the Simple Pleasures bakery, has a sushi bar and a simple dining room with about a dozen tables. It doesn't take reservations, which accounts for about the only criticism that can be leveled at the restaurant — it is too small.

Since it is also extremely popular, that means there is often a wait, and since there's no room to wait, that means you hover in the doorway getting under the feet of the waitstaff.

"Health Oriented Foods" is how Yama-Q bills itself, and this might deter some diners, just as the idea of tofu in broth deterred me. But if the food is healthful, that is a bonus; the important thing is that it is beautifully prepared and consistently delicious.

It is also a very good value, the only items that struck us as expensive being wine at $7 or $8 a glass. The menu is confusing until you know it better, because some of the appetizers — the duck quesadillas, for instance — and certainly the tempura plates ($6 to $9) are big enough for entrees.

The friendly and efficient waitstaff, dexterously navigating the close-packed room by some in-built radar, will warn you if you are ordering too much.

The menu for lunch is similar and take-out is available. Many people come just for the sushi, which is everything that sushi

should be, but on this occasion we decided to stick to the regular menu.

When ordering drinks at the beginning of the meal, you could ask for an order of edamame for the table — bright green fresh soybeans that are steamed in the shell. Instead of choosing a more conventional appetizer, strike out and order an unusual salad — a cucumber and wakame (bright green seaweed), hijiki (black seaweed), or burdock, a crisp root vegetable with a sweet, earthy flavor that was a great favorite in England in Elizabethan times.

Seafood dumplings ($6) tend to be shrimp, but at Yama-Q the shrimp was combined with fish in a felicitous union. The crab cakes ($9), a mix of snow crab, salmon, and onion, not only are among the crispest and lightest around, but have a distinctive flavor from some subtle spice.

An appetizer of the day was a green bean salad, lightly charred, mysteriously seasoned, the simplest of vegetables at its simple best.

Entrees are between $10 and $18, with some daily specials of steak or fish dishes in the low $20s.

Here again, it pays to be a little adventurous. Try buckwheat noodles and sauteed vegetables in a broth of kelp and shiitake mushrooms or brown rice and barley zousui, a hearty vegetarian stew. Not the first thing you'd pick, maybe, but both are excellent.

One of our more conventional diners chose the steak, clinging to the familiar food like a life raft in this sea of unusual vegetables and odd seafood, and very good it was, too. But the eel kabayaki, a very rich dish of steamed smoked eel over teriyaki vegetables and rice, was more interesting. Yama-Q's rice, whether brown or white or mixed with other grains, is exceptionally good.

A tuna fish kabob, on the other hand, was a little overcooked and lacked the zip of the other dishes.

The choice of tempura dishes was sweet potato, calamari, or shrimp and vegetable. We chose the latter, which, for a skimpy $9, gave you a plate of deep-fried heaven — a half dozen different vegetables and a generous handful of shrimp in a crisp light batter with no oily aftertaste.

Every dish is a stimulant to the palate, with interesting flavors in careful combinations, and the accompanying sauces and vegetables and relishes are different for each dish. A perfect advertisement that healthful eating doesn't have to be boring eating.

There is a big range of desserts. The banana tempura, served with whipped cream and fresh fruit, was out of this world, but we struck out on the orange cake, which was dry. The green tea ice cream was delicately flavored, not too sweet, cool and soothing. Ice cream and sorbet flavors vary, and have included ginger and mango, among others. A dairy-free brown rice pudding is served in a charming basket with a handle.

It's no secret that when it comes to eating, it's not necessarily the biggest and fanciest places that worm their way into your heart and become favorites. Yama-Q is definitely one of mine, a place to which I return again and again, even if sometimes there's an annoying wait.

December 2000

East Hampton & Springs

BABETTE'S

66 Newtown Lane

East Hampton

329-5377

Breakfast (until 5 PM), lunch, and dinner. Reservations only for six or more..

The décor at Babette's is 1950s Miami Beach, red and yellow and pale swimming pool blue, with funky lights and French posters. With windows on two sides, the place is full of light, which makes it a particularly cheery place for breakfast or lunch.

There is a small, sensibly priced wine list (though the wines by the glass are rather high), Pete's Wicked Ale, and an enormous list of fruit and vegetable juices, fruit smoothies, herbal teas, and other interesting beverages. I found the watermelon and lime juice as boring as all getout, but the hot chocolate — piled with whipped cream, chocolate sauce, and powdered chocolate — reduced a 6-year-old to awed good behavior.

The background music is a kind of pleasant easy-listening mix. "But it's not Muzak," said a musician in our party. "Listen. Those are good chord changes." I'll take his word for it.

Its rather spare look and tight seating give Babette's the feel of a funky diner, so its imaginative cooking, with a careful use of spices, comes as a surprise. It is a fun mixture of health food, Mexican, Indonesian, Californian, Chinese, and grassroots American and, while it is not inexpensive, neither is it exorbitant.

You can go the spinach juice/tofu burger route in spring, but during icy weather Babette's superlative chicken mole enchilada ($17.95) really hits the spot. Made with free-range chicken, tomatoes, red onions, smoked jalapenos, cheddar, and a great mole negra sauce, it comes with black beans, rice, salsa, perfectly ripe avocado, and sour cream.

We started our meal with one outstanding dish and one interesting dish. The grilled shrimp salad ($18.95) was expensive but great. The shrimp were smoky and full of flavor and really enhanced by a ginger and carrot sauce to dip them in. They came with plenty of avocado and mesclun with a chopped salad of jicama, carrot, apple, and tomato in the center of the plate.

For $12.95 there is a platter of parsleyed tabbouleh, little nutty falafel cakes, baba ganoush (mushed up eggplant), and a very good hummus, the whole accompanied by warm pita bread and a tiny salad of chopped black olives and tomato in a lettuce leaf. Many of the dishes have a small salad with them, each one a little different and each with a different dressing.

Two dishes chosen from the children's menu proved large enough for a hungry teenager. The veggie burger was huge and, though it was heavy on the lentils and looked a bit like organic compost, it was very nice. The toasted cheese sandwich was outstanding, cooked on a nutty brown bread and accompanied by a small bowl of fruit salad. Both dishes came with excellent sweet-potato fries.

One of our entrees was a daily special, chicken pot pie. While it had a good flaky crust, the filling was rather starchy and heavy on the root vegetables. A better choice was a featherlight Pad Thai, with slivers of chicken, shrimp, red and yellow peppers, and bean sprouts, with a spicy, but not intrusive, sauce ($19.95).

Many of these dishes are included in a $26.95 three-course prix fixe menu, which might be the way to go if you are hungry enough. Breakfast, which includes dozens of different omelettes, is served all day.

February 2004

BAMBOO

47 Montauk Highway

East Hampton

329-9821

Dinner seven days and Sunday brunch.

Bamboo, the elegant restaurant and sushi bar that took over an unlucky spot on Montauk Highway in East Hampton and completely dispelled the jinx, is now comfortably settled into the South Fork restaurant landscape. One of the things I enjoy about it is the way the tables are spread in a long curving line from the restrained taupe and celadon dining room down to the sizzling black and copper sushi bar. It means that the noise level is well-controlled and conversation does not become a shouting match. This does not apply if you turn up late on a summer weekend night, when the frenetic party scene would deafen a cactus.

We went to Bamboo on its big bargain-of-the-week night, Sunday, when all sushi is two portions for the price of one. This is good news for those who share sushi platters with loved ones and always get shortchanged. The faster-eating partner always pinches the one with the salmon roe or the best piece of eel, seems suddenly unable to accurately divide by two, and always ends with the question, "Aren't you going to finish that last one?" Bamboo's sushi is the epitome of freshness but the presentation is a little disappointing. One of the joys of sushi and sashimi is the gasp of astonishment it elicits when it arrives at the table looking like a work of art. The eye eats half the food.

While one of our diners went for the two-for-one sushi, two others opted for the $25 three-course prix fixe, a very good value. The menu is divided into "small plates," $7 to $12, and "large plates," $15 to $28. But many of those small plates, the highly recommended mussels, for example, are more than large enough to be an entree for most people. The miso soup — different from the conventional dish in having lobster wontons, tofu, and edamame — is really too big. I ordered it because, having arrived feeling really cold, I wanted hot soup to warm me. In this case, I could also have warmed myself by jumping into it and swimming a few

laps. The dim sum dumplings, prettily served in their bamboo steamer, were delicate and delicious. We tried three salads. The calamari salad with frisée and a vinaigrette of roasted yellow peppers and miso was excellent. Another, a grilled chicken teriyaki salad with napa cabbage chopped very finely and baby arugula, was pleasant but a little bland. The third was simply fabulous, a tuna and avocado salad with a mysteriously subtle dressing that tied the flavors and textures together to produce a winning goal. Wanting a spicy main course, I was advised to try the Bang Bang Chicken.

This turned out to be meltingly tender chicken in a sweet and spicy red glaze, served over Thai fried rice with a bit of broccolini for health's sake. It was very delicious in a rather old-fashioned, small-town Chinese restaurant way. As it turned out, the shiitake mushroom crusted salmon with stir fry vegetables was equally spicy. Now here is a dish to write home about. Every component was perfectly balanced. The highly flavored coating of chopped mushroom enlivened the perfectly cooked salmon without drowning its flavor.

The stir fry vegetables were spicily pungent while retaining a clean vegetable flavor. The udon noodle bowl, with noodles the size of sea snakes, small pieces of marinated beef, and plenty of mushroom, was a one-dish meal, hearty and satisfying. For best entree of the evening, I would have trouble choosing between the salmon and the grilled jumbo shrimp, served on a skewer, redolent with the flavor of lemongrass, and served over spinach surely grown in the Elysian Fields. The prix fixe people chose two desserts, a heavy but nicely flavored crème brûlée and a coconut rice pudding served with a lovely green tea ice cream. The coconut rice pudding? Totally weird.

Bamboo offers an exciting menu, fair prices, really pretty surroundings, a snappy bar for those who just come for the sushi and sashimi, and plenty of parking room. The place feels very welcoming, the service is a delight, and the food, with an occasional lapse, is very good.

April 2004

BLUE PARROT

33A Main Street

East Hampton

324-3609

Lunch and dinner, seven days. Seasonal. No reservations.

Mexican food has always been sort of a black hole in the Northeast. Sure there's Rosa Mexicana in Manhattan for those with deep pockets, but who among us hasn't heard about a great little place in Chicago where a meal for two costs $8.95 or tried the burritos rolled as thick as your forearm on a trip to San Francisco?

Heaven help those of us who have had a breakfast of chorizo sausage, fresh jalapeno peppers, and eggs in the great second-floor balcony of the central market in Guadalajara or tasted turkey in black mole sauce in the Yucatan.

No, us Yankees, particularly here on Long Island, have had to suffice with what is more appropriately called Mexican-theme food.

But in East Hampton of all places, tucking into a plump chicken tamale at the Blue Parrot, you can for a moment come close (especially if you ask for it without cheese). For that alone, the Blue Parrot ranks as a special place in a part of the world where restaurants are expensive whether they're good or not.

The Blue Parrot, run by a surfer who spends a good part of the year in Hawaii, doesn't take itself too seriously. The walls in the large front room are hung with signs of the "No Spurs, No Service" genre, while the back, smaller dining room is a shrine to the owner's passion: Surf photographs cover every square inch of wall space. A newly installed mock-adobe gas fireplace is supposed to add a homey touch, I guess, and gives you something else to look at when the room isn't full, which is not that often.

On weekends the crowd is often as much at the bar as at the tables, lined up three deep for the joint's brutal margaritas and selection of Mexican beers. The Blue Parrot bar is a point on the compass for the Stephen Talkhouse crowd and for obvious reasons is one of the world headquarters for Jimmy Buffett's Parrothead fans (a few of whom busted up the place the last time the singer performed hereabouts).

Given that vibe and the fact that the margaritas are downright dangerous — served over ice in one of those silly little glass jars with a handle — the staff has become adept at dealing with boisterous customers. A word to the wise: When the bartender at the Blue Parrot tells you you've had enough, you've had enough.

Despite all the goings-on at the bar, the food is able to command attention. This is a restaurant that doesn't pretend to greatness but what you get is satisfying and often imaginative.

The fried calamari ($8.95), a yardstick by which many restaurants should be judged, are not overly greasy and a have a nice mix of chili and other spices. The cilantro pesto dip they come with, a plug of chopped green resting forlornly at the bottom of a plastic cup of oil, could be better, however. Ask for another bowl of the salsa that is put on the table with the tortilla chips and dip your squid there.

Most of the appetizers are big enough for two, and the quite nice Mussels de la Casa, steamed over wine, onions, garlic, and cilantro ($9.95), is a bargain since the serving is big enough for three or more.

In all the years that I had been eating at the Blue Parrot, I had never noticed the Texas Toothpicks, a plate of deep fried onions and peppers hiding out at the bottom of the list of appetizers, until Saturday. How could this be? We tossed aside the onions and dug through the pile to get at every last spicy pepper strip.

"Are these jalapeno?" I asked a member of the waitstaff. "I don't know," she replied, adding that she didn't like spicy food.

Unfortunately, the Texas Toothpicks are just about the only item on the menu that comes with a kick (other than those knock-down margaritas). In general, the heat seems to have been set during the days of the Jimmy Carter White House.

The carnitas, grilled roasted pork chopped with garlic and onions, for example, could have used a little boot in the pants. Of course there is a bottle of hot sauce on every table, but there's no substitute for having the fire cooked right into the food.

The ceviche of scallops ($8.95), when they have it, which they did not on Saturday night, is a passable copy of those you'd get in a Mexican beach town. But if they're going to run out, why

not offer a ceviche, at least on occasion, using some of our fine local fish?

Since the Blue Parrot is up an alley opposite the East Hampton Cinema, and has relatively affordable meals and a rapid turn-around, the restaurant is an obvious choice for a pre-feature meal. On weekends, those in the know try to get a table just as the 7 p.m. movies are starting across the street.

If you are hungry and in a hurry, the huge fajita plates ($17.95 for chicken or beef, $18.95 for tuna) with monumental hunks of meat are a filling choice and will probably save you a few bucks on popcorn at the movies later.

A seafood fajita from the specials board, which on a recent night also featured blackened salmon and grilled pork chops, was nicely presented, but reminded one member of our party of a Chinese stir fry.

Most entrees come with a side of rice and black beans, which you either love or hate because of a mysterious mesquite flavor. Do I sense Liquid Smoke here? On the other hand, the black bean soup — sans fumet — is a solid, no-nonsense version of the old standard.

Another mystery is the $21 paella. While it's not bad, it's not exactly a Mexican dish or much of a paella either.

Happy surprises can be found on the menu though. The spinach and montrachet quesadilla ($14.95) was a pleaser to both the eye and the palate. Of course you wouldn't find this one South of the Border, but who cares?

The one dish that over the years has had me coming back again and again is the tuna burger ($14.95). It is often a struggle not to order this masterpiece of yellowfin tuna ground with onion, cilantro, and herbs served with a wasabi mayonnaise.

A lunch menu includes most of the dinner dishes and adds a fun eggplant sandwich for $7.95 and a grilled vegetable taco salad ($8.95) to the mix.

The other thing that you have to love about the Blue Parrot is the diversity among its customers. There are the obligatory swells from points west, young local families with kids squirming all over, and, on a recent Saturday, two separate tables of Latino workers enjoying a night out. Find that any place else in East Hampton.

March 2001

BOSTWICK'S

Harbor Marina, 39 Gann Road

East Hampton

324-1111

Dinner seven days. Lunch Saturday and Sunday. Seasonal.

Labor Day is not what it once was in terms of relief, but even so you could almost hear the communal sigh of relief at this one's end. The next day the sun came out and so did a lot of people who had been living like hermit crabs since Memorial Day.

These are the best months and an opportunity to enjoy an uncrowded outdoor meal, preferably one with a sunset and water view, before the South Fork's many seasonal restaurants close down.

One of these, next to the town commercial dock on Three Mile Harbor, is Bostwick's, an informal, friendly place that is a favorite spot for a drink after work, when the crowd spills out of the bar and down the outdoor stairs as the sun goes down. A sunset meal on its second-floor terrace has few equals for the view.

On the other side of the small boats in the marina is a busy waterway separating the shore from two small islands, one of which, Dayton Island, should you be looking for a pied-a-l'eau and have a couple of million dollars around, is for sale. Beyond them is the harbor and the sun setting over Hedges Banks.

On Friday there was a spectacular sunset and as it faded from the sky hundreds of tiny lights lit up on the ceiling of the covered terrace, echoing the stars that were popping into view one by one in the sky.

Bostwick's menu consists of tried and true favorites — clams and oysters on the half shell, lobsters and shellfish, chowder and fresh fish. Appetizers are $5 to $9; entrees $11 to $25, for half a crabmeat-stuffed lobster, flounder, baked oysters and clams, corn, and a baked potato.

There is an adequate wine list of reasonably priced bottles, and the beer on tap comes ice cold in iced mugs, which somehow seems to fit the ambience.

To my mind, the way to start your meal would be with six Robins Island oysters on the half shell ($8.95), but if you prefer your oysters cooked you can have them fried, Casino (with bacon and peppers), or Rockefeller (with spinach, shallots, and Parmesan cheese). We tried the latter, but they lacked molluscular magic.

The coconut chicken, pieces of chicken breast fried with a coconut crust and served on skewers with a delicious chunky mango chutney, was much more fun.

For an entree, you might choose a seafood pasta or the fish and chips, a hyper-crisp, battered cod with fries.

You might avoid the flounder ($18.95), which was surprisingly dull considering it was billed as local and must have been sparkling fresh. But dull as it was, the rice that accompanied it almost outdid it in dullness.

Hurry on to the big, fat crab cakes with great mashed potatoes and a generous pile of lovely baby asparagus, cooked so that there was still some crunch to them. The Key lime and mustard sauce is a bit dubious, but the crab cakes really don't need it.

Although Bostwick's obviously specializes in seafood, it does have salads and a few "shore dinners," ribeye steak ($21.95), duck ($18.95), chicken ($17.95), and what a number of people have told us is an excellent char-grilled hamburger and French fries for $10.95.

As an alternative to ordering from the entree side of the menu, the excellent mussels and steamers listed as an appetizer could be quite sufficient as a main course for most people.

For dessert, we loved the Key lime pie, which was super tart, but found the apple crumble rather soggy, though it did have a nice flavor, not overly sweet.

Bostwick's is full of fun, and the service is fast and friendly. Stick to the simpler dishes, but even if you choose a dish that wouldn't make it on "Iron Chef," with the water and the boats and the sunset you're not going to notice anyway.

September 2002

CAFE MAX

85 Montauk Highway

East Hampton

324-2004

Open for dinner and Sunday brunch;. Closed Tuesday.

Trendy is okay on occasion, elegant certainly has its moments, but for a satisfying evening you can't beat good food in a cozy and unpretentious setting.

Cafe Max can be found in a little dollhouse of a building on Montauk Highway that doesn't look big enough to hold a restaurant. But in the single high-raftered room there is enough space for a bar, more than a dozen tables, and a relaxed comfort duplicated by very few places.

The chef and owner, Max Weintraub, has been cooking on the East End since the glacial moraine was formed. While there are daily specials, he knows what works and what doesn't and the result is a medium-sized menu, heavy on fish, that has an immensely appealing selection.

It's definitely one of those menus where you are torn: If you have the sole with almonds and mango, that means you can't have lobster linguine; but if you have the lobster linguine you're going to miss out on the saffron fish stew.

There is a good selection of wines by the glass and an excellent wine list; though where they keep the wine I can't imagine (the cellar must really be in the cellar.)

Cafe Max is known for its friendly service, but it must be said that on this occasion our waiter was a little brisk with us and sometimes entered that waiterly nirvana where the waived arm becomes invisible to the naked eye, but high marks to another waiter who recognized a member of our party and brought the olive oil with garlic before she even asked.

Appetizers start at $5 for a soup or green salad and don't go above $9.50 (crab meat or shrimp cocktail). Pastas are $17 and entrees start at $17.50 for flounder and peak at $23 for an excellent rack of lamb. The average entree price is just under $20.

With the prices at East End restaurants mimicking the current heating oil gazumph, an average of $20 a plate for fine food is worth mentioning twice.

Black olives and good bread are brought to you as soon as you are seated, which is good because it must be said that service is leisurely. This is not a complaint, just advice in case you were thinking of catching a movie.

The lump crab meat, the most expensive appetizer, is perfectly fine, but you could have it at home. Try instead the crunchy crab cakes or, at only $6, a wonderful bruschetta with coarse peasant bread rubbed with garlic and olive oil and topped with seasoned chopped tomatoes and basil — a reminder that with good, simple ingredients you can't go wrong.

I had the roasted peppers with anchovies and goat cheese, which is what I had the last time and the time before that, because to my mind it is a perfect appetizer.

We also tried a special salad of the day with pear, walnuts, and Gorgonzola on mixed greens that ran a close second, beating by a nose a seared tuna sashimi with a nice smoky edge.

The veal Theresa — sauteed and served with a garlic and wine sauce with little shrimp on top — was as soft as butter and served with what I think is one of the best things on the menu, a wonderful, dark, herb-filled polenta.

A daily special of sea scallops was nice but quite outshone by the swordfish, served in a rather unusual thick wedge with peppercorns and mango vinaigrette, which was superlative.

"It's the best swordfish I have eaten in my life," said its recipient. A true compliment because, if I remember rightly, he's forever ordering swordfish.

We tried another special, coq au vin, which, while it was not traditional, being more baked than stewed, was a hit with everyone. All dishes came with nicely cooked vegetables, including good mashed potatoes and pureed yams.

It is perhaps one of Mr. Weintraub's signatures that he takes traditional dishes (like the coq au vin) and then dickers with them until they have his personal touch.

This showed in the desserts, particularly in the Key lime pie, which is very fluffy and light because Mr. Weintraub finds the traditional recipe too heavy. The strawberry shortcake, also, was as light as air, almost leaving the plate and floating away toward the ceiling.

Bargains to be noted: Max's offers prix fixe dinners nightly except Friday and Saturday from $18 to $21, a three-course Sunday brunch, and early bird specials every night. Pasta can be ordered in half portions (with meat, $8.50, without, $7.50).

February 2002

DELLA FEMINA

99 North Main Street

East Hampton

329-6666

Dinner seven days in summer. Closed Wednesday in winter.

Last weekend's perfect snowfall (three manageable inches dropped by an overnight storm) finally made it seem like winter. Up until then, about the only clue that the East End was in down time was the arrival of a flurry of prix fixe menus, that single sheet slipped inside the high-priced à la carte folder that spells a gastronomic break for year-rounders.

This year, more restaurants than ever seem to be offering bargains — free wine here, two-for-ones there — but for sheer value few can beat Della Femina's three-course $24 prix fixe.

Each of the three courses offers three choices and the menu also offers a red or a white California wine at $6 a glass, which is good because the wine list tends toward the expensive and bottled water will set you back $7.50.

We tried two $25 red wines, a Deshenrys Fauges from the Languedoc and a Bedell merlot and, much though I like to push local wines, the former was a clear winner.

Della Femina is a very attractive restaurant, and not just for those who step in through the doors and shell out their lima beans for a meal. Even if you never set foot inside, the green wreaths against the hunter green paint at Christmas and the overflowing window boxes in the summer are a downright public service.

Inside, all is discreet good taste — soft lights, cream walls, beige carpet — to such an extent it almost makes you nervous. What is this, a shoot for Wallpaper magazine? You look around desperately for a mural of Positano, a raffia-covered chianti bottle, any bit of bad taste.... Aaah...! With relief you spot the wall of caricatures; more than enough Hamptons celebrity-worshiping flimflam there to scratch that particular itch.

Bless them for the carpet. On Friday night every table was taken and it was very noisy, but without the carpet it would have been so much noisier. Our waitress told us that some restaurants actually put foam rubber on the undersides of the tables and chairs to help with the noise problem. It's a vicious circle: You can't hear, you raise your voice, so does everyone else, and you end up with a room full of shouting people.

By the time we ordered, the kitchen was out of the fried local squid with a Thai dressing, which would have been a disappointment except that we would then have missed the exceptional salad of Roquefort, endive, melon, bacon, candied pecans, and lamb's lettuce that was the substitute.

Elizabeth David, in her classic book "French Provincial Cooking," wrote that the main object of an hors d'oeuvre is to provide something so beautifully fresh it arouses your appetite and puts you in good spirits. This salad certainly met those criteria. While all the fancy bits and pieces in the salad were grand, it was the frothy bundle of lamb's lettuce, so fresh it almost bounced on the plate, that sent the spirits soaring.

The green salad, sprinkled with tiny tomatoes, was fine, but while $11 for the Roquefort salad didn't raise an eyebrow, $9 for the green salad was pushing it a bit. The other prix fixe appetizer was a white bean soup with greens and sausage. Thick enough to qualify as a stew, the soup was elevated from blandness by the excellent sausage.

The last time I ate here, there was a wonderful asparagus risotto with duck confit and white truffle oil on the menu, and I was glad to see it still there ($12), though not on the prix fixe. It was just as good this time.

Get a bad risotto (and chances are you'll meet one on the East End sooner rather than later) and you won't want to try it again. But when the flavors meld happily and the rice is perfect it is a really knockout dish.

The one entree we tried from the à la carte menu sounded good — monkfish wrapped in jamon serrano, a Spanish cured ham — but the ham and the accompanying celery puree and vegetables were not enough to breathe life into the fish, which tasted as if it had died of boredom.

The two fish dishes on the prix fixe were a different matter: an exemplary miso and sake-glazed salmon with wonderful scallion mashed potatoes and a halibut whose flavor, although delicate, was there with bells on. All the dishes were beautifully

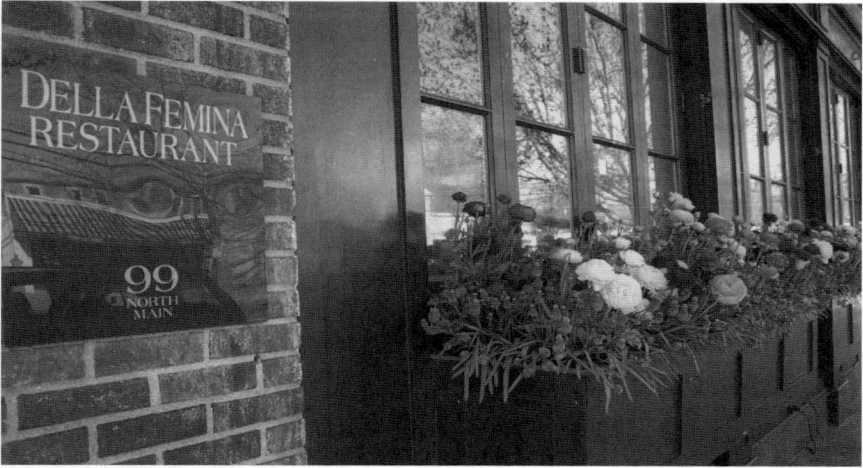

presented, but the halibut (so exclusive it was caught on a day boat in Maine) looked particularly pretty with its crown of frizzled leeks.

Then there was a fine muscular dish of garganelli pasta with shrimp and a rich tomato and caramelized onion sauce which would have satisfied the most hearty post-sledding appetite.

But the diner who selected the grilled hanger steak struck out; it was so tough as to be almost inedible.

Let's draw a veil over that and move on to the desserts, which is where the diner really scores because they are made in house and are a far cry from the slice of apple pie or cheesecake the average prix fixe might include.

I particularly recommend the dense chocolate espresso pot au crème, served with a scoop of chocolate gelato and chocolate sauce, though the crème brûlée was almost as good. The polenta mascarpone tart, as its name suggests, was not quite so exciting, despite the candied kumquats and pecan tuile, but satisfying nonetheless.

The last time I reviewed this restaurant was in 1998, and it was interesting to find many of the same dishes on the menu. This time the service was faster and friendlier while the quality of the food seemed off a little. But there is no doubt that it is still very good — and the prix fixe, as I said, is a real bargain.

January 2002

EAST HAMPTON POINT

295 Three Mile Harbor-Hog Creek Road

East Hampton

329-2800

Dinner seven days. Lunch Monday through Saturday. Seasonal.

Reservations two weeks in advance.

While all restaurants work hard to achieve fame through the merits of their food and service, there are some that steal ahead, start over the competition because of a wonderful natural setting — and East Hampton Point is one of them. There is no hint of a view as you drive up to the front entrance, but as you walk in the waters of Three Mile Harbor are laid out before you.

This has the most amazing tonic effect. You breathe a big sigh and, if the weather is kind and you have had the sense to arrive some time ahead of your reservation, wander out onto the bar's huge deck. There you can sip a Pernod or a Dubonnet, or something else that makes you feel as if you are in Europe, and watch boats docking for the evening as the sun goes down.

You can also eat outdoors rather more casually, and less expensively, on the deck. The menu is simple, with hamburgers and fish and chips, but there are some more sophisticated choices as well. For a casual summer lunch or dinner before the movies, it is a great deal.

No one was sitting on the deck on Friday evening, which was as damp and miserable as Memorial Day itself, but the restaurant was fairly hopping, with a holiday crowd that seemed to be talking at the top of its collective lungs. Just for a few minutes toward sunset, the clouds lifted a little, and an orange band of sky was reflected in the water of the harbor. It would be nice to say that the diners hushed to observe the beauty of the moment — but everyone was talking too much to notice.

Appetizers presented a good mix of the traditional and the more adventurous. The clam soup was simplicity itself. While many such soups taste of just about anything but clams, the mollusks' redolence rose up from the bowl and floated across the table at East Hampton Point. Clams on the half shell, which should per-

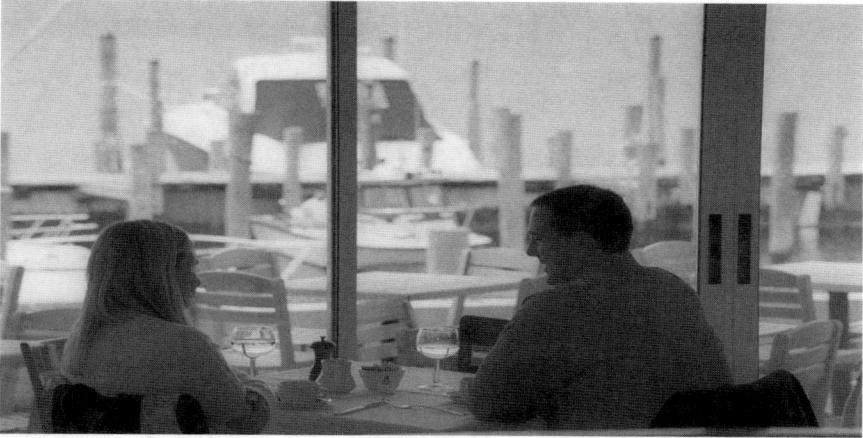

haps be an obligatory item on East End menus, were also available.

The crab cakes were terrific — crab cakes really seem to be looking up on the East End — with the outer coating crispy, but very thin, and not at all oily.

Perhaps the most interesting of the appetizers we tried was the cold tuna tart — small slices of rare tuna, marinated and seared on the outside, served on top of a slightly spicy tuna tartare.

The dressing on the simple green salad was judged a little too sweet by two members of our party, but the other two thought it just right — so who can say?

As for the entrees, the choice of lamb shanks was perhaps a mistake on an early summer day; the dish just seemed a bit too hearty. A great big helping in a rich sauce, piled with light, crispy noodles, the lamb shanks would be a meal to purr over on a cold December night, but on this occasion, they were daunting, and the call for the doggy bag was heard in the land.

One of the evening's specials was pasta in a light marinara cream sauce. It was proof that the simplest dish can often be the best. With fresh pasta, fresh ingredients, the very best Parmesan floating in slivers on the top, it received rave reviews from its recipient, who deemed it rich but light, and was quite reluctant to pass it across to the reviewer for a taste test.

Our other two choices were fish — skate and halibut, which presented an interesting contrast in both presentation and the idea behind them: the nun versus the overpainted floozie with rhinestones on her sweater and too much jewelry.

The halibut was served completely plain, with some beautifully cooked mussels and a piece of baked fennel. Again, the verdict is so much a matter of personal preference — the flavor of the halibut, merely enhanced a little by the juice from the fennel, seemed delicate perfection to one of us, but another wanted sauce.

Then there was the skate, a dream of a fish when cooked properly in, say, a little blackened butter with caper sauce, but often a rubbery disaster. Well, East Hampton Point's skate is just right, tender and, well, just right. But for some unimaginable reason it came served up on a bier of what looked like my Auntie Muriel's home fries, greasy cubes of ham and fried potato that interfered with the taste of the skate, until they were carefully scraped to one side of the plate. Scratch those next time.

Everything was beautifully served, but the desserts were ethereal. The crème brûlée could not have been improved upon, and a little sculpted castle of fresh berries with crème anglaise on a light pastry crust was tart and refreshing — but there was a concoction of caramelized bananas with banana ice cream on the menu that was so good we nearly ordered another portion.

A big restaurant demands a high degree of efficiency, and East Hampton Point seems to achieve it without the attendant loss of gaiety among the wait crew that often results. They are a upbeat bunch, and on Friday night, the beginning of the season, seemed endearing because each waiter was trailed by a trainee, learning the ropes.

It's by no means a quiet evening out at East Hampton Point — the noise level is intense at times. Nor is it an inexpensive one: The meal came to about $65 a head, including an excellent, smoky, light red Terra Rosa cabernet sauvignon which was on the low end of the price list at $25. But you feel that it has been a special occasion — the beautifully presented food, the friendly service, and, of course, the view.

June 2000

JAMES LANE CAFE

At the Hedges Inn, 74 James Lane

East Hampton

324-7100

Dinner seven days.

As we arrived at the James Lane Cafe on Sunday night, there were two deep tire marks running from Woods Lane across the grass at the end of Town Pond, across James Lane, over the fence, across the restaurant's lawn, and through beds of honeybell hostas right up to the edge of the dining terrace.

Someone had been in a real hurry! Was this, we wondered, an omen that a good meal was ahead of us? And, even though we discreetly used the parking lot instead of driving directly into the dining room, the answer was yes.

The wine list at James Lane Cafe has a lot of variety, but prices are high. Wines by the glass also tend to be pricey — buying by the bottle is the way to go — but there was a very pleasant Chilean merlot for $6.50.

Appetizers range from $6 for chilled seafood gazpacho to $12 for sauteed shrimp. Entrees start at $16 for crab cakes, are under $25 for most dishes, then jump to $28 to $30 for steaks, veal and lamb chops, and lobster.

While there was a bit of a wait between courses, the service was efficient and thoughtful. The James Lane Cafe, unlike many places, serves hot food on extremely hot plates. Too hot to touch, in fact. But our waitress carried them to the table without gloves. How did she do it? We award her the Asbestos Finger Prize.

In the summer, the restaurant doubles its size by opening an outdoor dining tent, a romantic place with a stone-flagged floor and a pleasant breeze. There were four of us sitting at a rather large round table and the room was full, but we could carry on a conversation without raising our voices.

We started our meal with an excellent $7 Caesar salad with nice crunchy garlic croutons and some excellent fried calamari with a light, crisp batter coating. This dish is memorable for having received the only criticism we could come up with all evening — the tomato dipping sauce was rather bland.

One of the evening's specials was a plate of sashimi-style tuna and scallops, topped with caviar. The tuna and scallops had the consistency and oily translucency of gravlax and a wonderful flavor, which was enhanced by the salty roe. Lovely.

But for real value, we recommend the seafood gazpacho. If you grow your own tomatoes, you may feel by now that if you see another one you'll scream, but the divine, ripe, late summer tomato is only with us for a short while and in January you'll look back to missed opportunities with regret.

This gazpacho is one such opportunity — sweet, zingingly fresh, with just a little peppery punch, and laced with shrimp, scallops, and crab meat.

We doubted that the entrees could be as good. The rack of lamb, at $29, was the most expensive dish we tried. It came with a delicious herb crust and some of the best garlic mashed potatoes around.

On the less expensive end of the meal, a large dish of penne with asparagus, fresh and sun-dried tomatoes, garlic, and lots of shrimp was worth every penny of $18.

With salmon being served in all sorts of fancy ways these days, James Lane chooses to serve it poached in an herb broth. Sound dull? Don't you believe it. It was subtly, delicately wonderful. And as for the lobster corn cakes, another of the specials, they were bliss.

Well, now it was time for dessert, which is where many restaurant flag and collapse just before they reach the finish line. We were going to catch them here, we were certain.

We ordered a crème brûlée and a Key lime pie. The crème brûlée had just the lightest of caramelized coatings (too many crème brûlées look like that scene from "Alexander Nevsky" when the German invaders fall through the foot-thick ice). The underlying custard was cool and smooth and suffused with just the right amount of vanilla.

The Key lime pie had a wonderful crumbly crust (and this on a very damp evening) and a filling that was an edible song. Do I wax poetic? You bet.

"Everything is wonderful. I almost feel like ordering another dish to see if we can't find something wrong," said one of our guests. But we knew that it was game, set, and match to the James Lane Cafe.

"I know — tell them the water was very run-of-the-mill."

August 2000

JEAN-LUC EAST

103 Montauk Highway
East Hampton
324-1100
Dinner seven days. Late bar menu on weekends.

Ever since the giant letters JL appeared outside, there has been a great deal of curiosity about Jean-Luc East, the restaurant that has taken over a large building just west of East Hampton Village.

It seems that every time this restaurant changes hands it is revamped from the bottom up, and this time is no exception. The main dining room with its monster bar was once painted black. It is now bright and light and, in keeping with its rather barnlike space, furnished with oversize accessories — a row of palm trees and huge glass vases filled with bird-of-paradise flowers, giant ficus leaves, and other exotic foliage.

The rear dining room has soft lighting, dark walls, and banks of mirrors. There is also an outdoor patio and bar that is breathtakingly attractive, with lots of red brick, French cafe chairs, a vine-covered pergola strung with small lights in rattan covers, and a barrier of conifers and exuberant flowers that completely shuts out the noise from the highway.

It is definitely one of the most attractive restaurants on the South Fork, maybe the most attractive. But while it is chic, chic, chic, it's not the country. It's the Hamptons as seen through the eyes of Manhattan.

The number of staff is amazing. When we arrived, there were four handsome young men standing in the driveway, another materialized in the parking lot to open the car door, and yet another opened the door to the restaurant. There were no less than five good-looking young women standing at the desk clutching menus. The place looked overstaffed, although by the end of the evening we could understand why.

We were offered a choice between dining inside or out and were delighted to get a table on the patio. There was some quiet, mellow music, though when we complimented our waitress on this she advised us that it was likely to change during the evening.

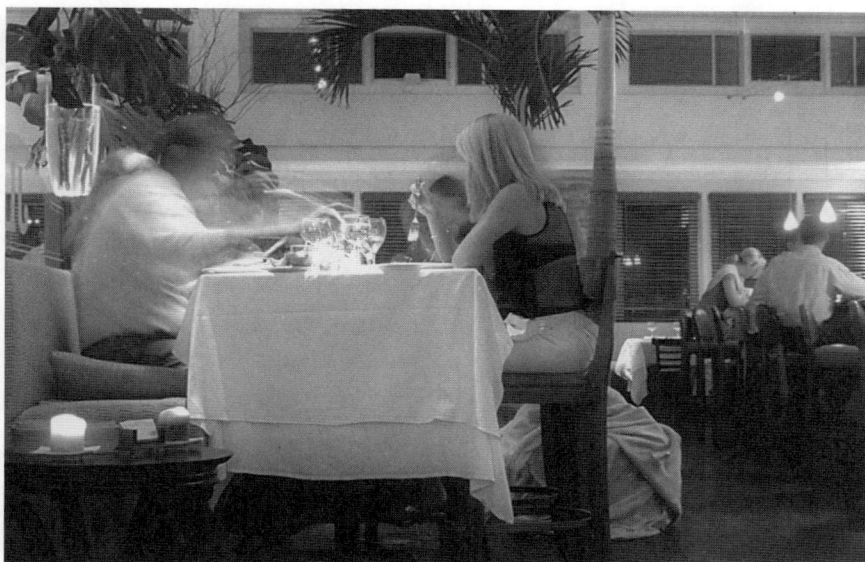

And so it did. Gradually the volume increased, and the bass beat crept in, and the restaurant slowly morphed from an elegant dining experience into a scene. By the time we left at 10, they were standing six deep at the bar. The bright blue lichee martinis were flashing past, and the whole place was in deep party mode, although the dress code was rather more Massapequa than Manhattan.

And this is the moment to state quite clearly, because I've probably been giving you the wrong idea, that JL is less expensive than you might expect. Appetizers are $7 to $16, entrees $19 to $29. There is an impressive raw bar, which includes ceviche ($9) maki rolls ($13), tuna tartare and caviar ($12), shrimp cocktail ($15), and lobster cocktail ($17), in addition to clams and oysters.

The wines are expensive, with only a couple of bottles under $30. But the list is carefully chosen — the Castle Rock merlot we picked, at $29 the cheapest red available, was better than many a more expensive wine elsewhere.

Of the four appetizers we tried, the scallop ceviche won hands down. It was a perfect balance of taste and texture, and just the right size as not to overwhelm. The "Georgica Beach crab cake" ($12) (no, alas, the crab actually comes from Alaska) was very good and was served on a bed of black beans and avocado, mixed with spiced mayonnaise and chive oil that was extremely imaginative, as, indeed, were all the accompaniments.

Lobster and vegetable spring roll ($16) was the most expensive appetizer on the list, but, while crisp and very pleasant, not a patch on the crab cake. We also tried a daily special of fried oysters where, in the battle between breadcrumbs and oysters, the breadcrumbs had won.

We thought $27 was a very good price for a big, perfectly cooked sirloin steak that arrived with enough fries for an army. The fries were standard but the steak was terrific.

The very good Colorado lamb chops ($29) were also a quite generous portion. They came with some stringy broccoli rabe and a wonderful parsnip gratin that was one of the best things we had all evening.

The baked halibut is highly recommended, gently cooked, with a crunchy crab meat crust. It too came with an exciting accompaniment, in this case a mixture of couscous, tomato, and fennel — great flavor!

The other entree we tried was paella, a dish I am inclined to be a little exigent about, having lived in Spain for a decade or so. It is an extremely difficult dish to do well. This one was full of good stuff, particularly the all-essential saffron, but the rice was too wet and the chicken too dry.

Jean-Luc shone in the dessert department. The two we tried, a caramelized banana crepe and a pear tarte Tatin, were amazingly good.

One note about service. Our waitress was so adorable that when she brought two glasses of Montrachet with dessert instead of Muscat de Barms de Venise that had been ordered, we decided not to say anything. But obviously something must have felt wrong, because five minutes later she came rushing back with the right after-dinner drinks. As far as we could judge, all the waitstaff were equally enthusiastic and anxious to please.

August 2003

THE LAUNDRY

31 Race Lane

East Hampton

324-3199

Dinner seven days.

With the South Fork looking like a location shoot for "Nanook of the North" for the past couple of weeks, everyone has been staying close to home; even visiting Inuits were probably snacking on seal blubber sandwiches in front of their own log fires. So, for those hardy souls who had eaten all their supplies and felt like going out to a restaurant, only somewhere extremely warm and inviting would induce them to harness up the black Lab sled team and set out into the cold.

The Laundry was probably high on the list. From the blast of an overhead heater's hot air thawing you out as you enter to a blazing log fire surrounded by big fat sofas, the place is welcome personified. Add friendly service, an unintimidating bar, and a suit-all-moods menu, which means you can eat as grandly or as simply as you want — spend a lot or spend a little — and you know why the Laundry is such a favorite.

Apart from a brief spell of madness when someone, no doubt a Manhattan marketing expert, painted its beautiful stripped red brick walls gray, took away the sofas, and doubled the portions and the fat content, the Laundry has remained very much the same. The prices have hardly changed since I last visited on duty two and a half years ago, and the menu is still stimulating, though not quite as mix-and-match experimental as it once was.

The appetizers start at $6 for soup and rise to $15 for crab cakes. Most of them can be ordered as an entree, but be warned that the appetizer size makes a perfectly adequate main dish. Certainly the entree portion of baby back ribs was too much for one person, good though it was.

Salads are $6 to $11. Entrees start at $15 for a burger with — drum roll, please — the Laundry's superlative French fries. I have this skinny size-four friend who is obsessed with French fries (yes, life is unfair) and I have her word for it that the Laundry's fries are the best on the East End. Pastas are around $17 and most dishes are under $25, with an aged sirloin steak being the most expensive at $34.

There is a $28 three-courses-plus-coffee prix fixe served Sunday through Friday with choices among nearly everything on the menu. This is an obvious bargain for those prepared to eat their way from soup to nuts. Though it seems to be okay to order two appetizers for your meal, note that there is an $8 charge for splitting an entree.

Let's start with the salads, not a subject to get me panting with excitement unless it is midsummer, but the Laundry has a baby spinach concoction ($10) that is out of this world. It has the ubiquitous combination of pear, nuts, and goat cheese, but what sets it apart is that the pears are lightly grilled and warm and the nuts are pistachios rather than walnuts. The Caesar salad ($8) would have been fine but it was icy cold — it gave me an ice cream headache.

The other interesting salad ($11) offers a hearty mixture of frisée, poached egg, bacon lardons, and red onion. It was very good, but it was edged out by the baby spinach. That '50s favorite, a wedge of iceberg lettuce with a thick dressing ($6), is back in vogue again, but I'll pass, thanks.

If you like mussels, try them in a Thai red curry broth ($7), particularly good on a cold winter night. The ricotta and butternut squash ravioli ($8), served with arugula and crisp sprinklings of prosciutto, were satisfying in the creamy, comforting way of mashed potatoes or rice pudding.

You can't really go wrong with a Laundry hamburger, but it won't surprise you. For that, you have to go with the amazingly tender and tasty barbecued ribs, which had everyone at the table oohing and aahing — and there were still leftovers to take home.

One of the specials on the day we were there was a weather-appropriate pork tenderloin with roasted vegetables, mashed potatoes, and a thick, rich gravy ($18). It, too, was extremely good, as is one of the Laundry's signature dishes, the sautéed calf's liver ($21) with caramelized onions, bacon, and more of those garlic mashed potatoes. Liver lovers, used to battling the world in defense of their favorite dish, are a loyal but demanding crew. The Laundry can face the most exigent of them without a blush.

Our token dessert was a delicious brownie, topped with ice cream and chocolate sauce, for only $4. Hey! What happened to that sticky toffee pudding and the steamed lemon pudding? Bring 'em back!

March 2003

THE MAIDSTONE ARMS

207 Main Street

East Hampton

324-5006

Breakfast, lunch, and dinner seven days.

Sprawled on a rise overlooking Town Pond, the Maidstone Arms is the closest thing to an old-fashioned New England inn that the Hamptons has to offer.

It is a pleasure to climb the steps and look out across the meadow to South End Cemetery and the pond. There could be yellow flag iris by the water, or the kousa dogwoods in bloom, or swans nesting. Once I saw an osprey swoop low over the pond and grab a golden carp so large that the bird barely cleared the trees as it took off.

Of course, you have to grab these quiet moments when you can because there is usually nose-to-tail hellish traffic pounding past, belching diesel fumes and stopping for no man.

But the inside of the inn is always tranquil. There is a bar, but its clientele seems a contemplative lot. There are no 35-year-olds in miniskirts and Sex-in-the-City heels screaming with laughter at the jokes of beefy arbitragers with Porsches. The two dining rooms are carpeted and quiet and people do not have to strain to make themselves heard.

Of course some might say that the inn is a little too hushed, a bit staid, a safe bet to take your Aunt Hettie on her birthday but not a hot date that you hope will get hotter. But by August, when everyone is desperate for a bit of quiet relaxation, they will be singing a different song.

The big change in the last couple of years is the addition of a "Boat Bar and Bistro" menu, which is less expensive than the dining room menu. The Inn also offers a choice of two prix fixes, one at $25 and the other $50, on occasion.

This means that although the list of wines by the glass may give you sticker shock — one, an excellent shiraz, is $7, but all the rest are $10 and up — your bill at the end of the meal could be, as ours was, quite reasonable. We were four: One ordered prix fixe,

one ordered two appetizers, one ordered from the bar menu, and another ordered from the dining room menu.

Of the two salads we tried, the $14 lump crab with tomatoes and avocados was the more exciting, but the big plateful of lolla rosa lettuce with blue cheese and balsamic roasted Vidalia onions made for a refreshing salad — though for $10 they could have thrown in a few more of the delicious onions.

The soup of the day, a clam chowder with a tomato base, was the only disappointment of the meal. It was bland, dull. Here in chowder central you have to look to your laurels when there are so many good chowders available.

The sauteed red snapper is highly recommended. The fish was perfect and came accompanied by a lovely mixture of fiddlehead ferns, snap peas, haricots verts, and little red and yellow pear tomatoes. "Crispy flattened free range chicken" was a bit ho-hum but rescued by a baby vegetable ragout that was masterful.

A dish that was really special, and out of the ordinary, was the seared sea scallops with white truffle oil. They arrived on a bed of bright green risotto, larded with tiny fresh peas. The mixture of textures and tastes was most successful.

Cataplana is a seafood stew with a difference: the usual prawns, mussels, and clams with a tomato-based sauce enlivened by the addition of fennel and spicy Mergueze sausage.

The Maidstone Arms is one place where the desserts won't be a disappointment. Although they include the ubiquitous crème brûlée, this one was a crème de la crème brûlée and as for the chocolate Napoleon — a featherlight concoction of chocolate mousse sandwiched between slivers of the lightest chocolate-flavored pastry possible — it was mind-boggling.

There are two things that stand out about the Maidstone Arms. One is that the ambience, service, and presentation give a meal a special-occasion feel. The other is that it is a very professional place and, come drought or blizzard or a second Bush term, you can rely on it.

May 2004

MARY JANE'S

128 North Main Street

East Hampton

324-8008

Lunch and dinner seven days. Sunday brunch. Takeout.

If you are going out to dinner in East Hampton Village, the problem is too many choices, not too few. But lunch, that's another matter.

If what you have in mind is somewhere inexpensive, with interesting food, comfortable surroundings, and friendly service, somewhere cozy but sunny, elegant but not too formal, then your choices are pretty limited.

So here's some good news: Mary Jane's on North Main Street has just started serving lunch, and it meets all those requirements.

Each time I have eaten at night at Mary Jane's, the restaurant has been a little prettier. Now there is a delightful bar with big chintz sofas, Oriental rugs, and a fireplace. There is another fireplace in the main dining room, and books and flowers everywhere. As the South Fork is gradually subsumed into suburbia, Mary Jane's country inn atmosphere makes one feel downright nostalgic.

And, bless them, Mary Jane's has carpet instead of tiles, which means that the acoustics are great and you won't have to shout.

When we were there on a Friday, the dining room was not only cozy but full of sunlight. The logs crackled in the fireplace (in truth it was one of those artificial grates, but you would be hard put to tell it from the real thing) and lunch was served with a proper tablecloth.

There are four categories on the lunch menu — appetizers, soups and salads, fresh pasta, and sandwiches — but any dish makes an adequate lunch, particularly because the meal starts with what might be considered a course of its own, Mary Jane's famous garlic rolls. Encrusted with bits of garlic and dripping in oil, they send the calorie indicator ricocheting off the scale and are completely irresistible.

Prices start at $3 for a cup of soup. Appetizers, which include mussels, fried calamari, crab cake, crostini, and an artichoke and spinach dip with chips, are $5 to $7.

There is a platter of olives, poached pears, candied figs, and cheeses for $9, vegetarian antipasto for $8, salads for $6, or a variety of pasta dishes between $10 and $12.

The sandwiches include various wraps, burgers, pizzas, quesadillas, and an open-faced pot roast sandwich, all either $8 or $9.

Many of the dishes are included on Mary Jane's all-day lounge menu for those who want something to eat when they drop in for a late morning cappuccino or a snack after the movies. There is also a popular $14.95 Sunday brunch, with pancakes and omelets made to order, ham, smoked salmon, fruit, and desserts.

We tried a big plate of hot, spicy seafood gumbo, served New Orleans style with lots of shrimp, crawfish, oysters, okra, and andouille sausage, which was not only very good but a bargain at $6.

One of the appetizers was an extremely tender chicken satay, which made a perfectly adequate main course because it was served with a small salad of greens and chopped tomato. The spicy peanut sauce that came with it, though a little ambiguous in flavor, packed a fierce peppery punch that opened the sinuses — I liked that.

Wraps are usually stodgy, leaden, and to be avoided. But the one we tried at Mary Jane's, made with portobello mushrooms, roasted peppers, field greens, daikon radish sprouts, and a roasted garlic and white bean hummus paste — flavors that complemented rather than canceled out — was fresh and juicy and light.

The linguine with clams in a red sauce (not heavy red sauce but a light, fresh tomato red sauce) was very nice and almost too big a serving for lunch time.

The unanimous favorite of the table was a delicious and unusual ravioli stuffed with a sweet butternut squash and served in an Amaretto and pistachio cream sauce. Its sweetness made it fall into some new category midway between entree and dessert.

For five of us, each of whom had a tea or coffee, the bill, before tip but including tax, came to $58, or just over $11 each. Can't complain about that.

Between rushing from one table to another, our waitress apologized for the service not being as fast as it could be. It seems that the restaurant had been taken completely by surprise by getting a full house for lunch so soon. Evidently the word is out.

November 2002

MICHAEL'S AT MAIDSTONE

28 Maidstone Park Road

East Hampton

324-0725

Dinner seven days.

When the news came in that Dennis MacNeil, formerly of Peconic Coast and before that of the Laundry, was now cooking at Michael's, home of the prime rib special and the freestanding chalk board, it aroused interest.

Was Michael's going upscale? Would the patterned wallpaper and Victoriana be replaced by white walls and tile floors? Would the prices skyrocket?

So at the first opportunity, The Star's reviewing crew set off to find out. The first thing we discovered, after two of us got lost and arrived 15 minutes late, is that Michael's still holds the record for hardest-to-find restaurant on the East End.

It was very reassuring to find that this East Hampton stalwart, this bastion against the I'm-entitled-to-be-rude crowd, looks just the same, from the sleepy, penumbrous bar to the cozy booths, pink glow, and tchotchkes in the dining room.

The wine list remains as it was — a sensible number of very reasonably priced wines, including a nice Stonehaven shiraz at $23. The menu is completely different, surf 'n' turf is out, salmon croquettes are in. But it is still reasonably priced, with all the main course specialties — and they are the way to go — being under $20.

Service at Michael's, usually zippy, was like molasses at our table, though a friend who ate there the next night reported quite the opposite. But then she had Michael's famous busboy who moves at the speed of light.

I am going to talk about the entrees first, because they are divided into two different sections, two different ways of eating, one of which is a bit weird.

We tried three main course specialties, all of which were excellent, well-balanced, carefully prepared dishes. Dishes that you wouldn't get at home.

The sautéed calf's liver with a rich red wine and vinegar sauce and rice pilaf ($17.50) was perfection. If you are a fan of liver, and I am, it doesn't get better than this. There was also a luscious pork tenderloin ($18.95) in a spicy, soy-based sauce. We could also have chosen duck or chicken or a burger with fries ($11.95).

Three pizzas are offered at $11.95 and four pastas at $15.95. We tried the freshly made linguine with a Bolognese sauce and found that although it was laden with sauce it was surprisingly light and flavored with subtlety. No red sauce nightmare here.

But then there was "Michael's Custom Dining," a choice of three seafood and four meat dishes served unaccompanied. It said that on the menu, but we didn't realize just how unaccompanied that was, without even a garnish. Believe me, nothing looks so naked as a few lonely sea scallops on a large plate.

We realized that you not only had to order a vegetable and a starch, but also a sauce. The scallops were $17.95, a sauce would have been $3, a baked potato $2, which brings it to $22.95.

The vegetables, fries, rice, or mashed potato only come in family sizes, from $5 to $7.50, so add a share of the family-sized spinach we ordered and it comes to nearly $25. Now we are not looking so inexpensive.

The salmon, at $14.50 for a nice piece, seemed a good value, but a New York strip steak at $26 is going to set you back $30-plus once you start adding stuff.

And then there is the matter of the sauces. Would curry-coconut go well with the Chatham codfish? With the rack of lamb? How about a merlot sauce with the salmon? Who knows? You'd much rather put your faith in the chef. I don't know, maybe diners like to do it this way. But it looked a bit daft to me.

To get back to the beginning of the meal, appetizers are more expensive than they used to be, but also more imaginative. There is a choice among five salads, five shellfish dishes, and five specialties. Prices range from $6.50 for a green salad to $11.50 for grilled shrimp.

We tried three, and unanimously recommend the calamari grilled Portuguese style, which had so much more character and essential squiddiness than those battered and deep-fried fellows. Also first rate were the little salmon croquettes with a saffron and roast pepper sauce and a soothing salad of red and yellow beets with some nicely contrasting red onion marmalade and a peppy walnut and horseradish sauce.

Despite some confusion, it's good to see Michael's branching out and doing something a bit different. The place is just as welcoming but the food is more adventurous.

April 2003

NICHOL'S

Montauk Highway

East Hampton

324-3939

Breakfast, lunch, and dinner seven days. Reservations only for large parties.

When I reviewed Nichol's a few years ago, shortly after it had moved into the little shack that had been the Quiet Clam since John Howard Payne was in town, one of the things I mentioned was the generous portions of the wines by the glass.

Prices have risen a little, but the glasses could still hold an inebriated goldfish in comfort. But this time I'm not reporting on the good value of the wine, but of the food.

While I have been to Nichol's many times for lunch or breakfast, because I have a son who is hooked on their eggs Benedict, I haven't been there for dinner in years, even though I live only a stone's throw away.

What's this, I thought, pork chops for $13? Scallops, salmon, or tuna for the same price? Seafood pie or chicken pot pie for $12? Filet mignon for $19? Are we in a time warp?

And although the wines by the glass — the shiraz and cabernet sauvignon are recommended — are an attraction, the beers are even more interesting. At Nichol's you can find Boddingtons and Guinness on tap, Fuller's London Pride and Newky Brown (Newcastle Brown Ale), not to mention Irish cider. The owners are English. Did you guess?

The interior is decorated with cows, sandblasted glass lamps, attractive photos on the wall, and flowers everywhere. I am neurotically averse to loud music in restaurants, but if you are a child of the 1960s I absolutely defy you not to have melted and given in to the owners' selections by the end of the evening. The Everly Brothers, The Beatles, Sam Cooke, Otis Redding, The Moody Blues, all the best songs from the days before pop music went down the tubes.

When the weather is fine, there is a pretty patio outside where you can relax and count the S.U.V.s as they race along Montauk Highway.

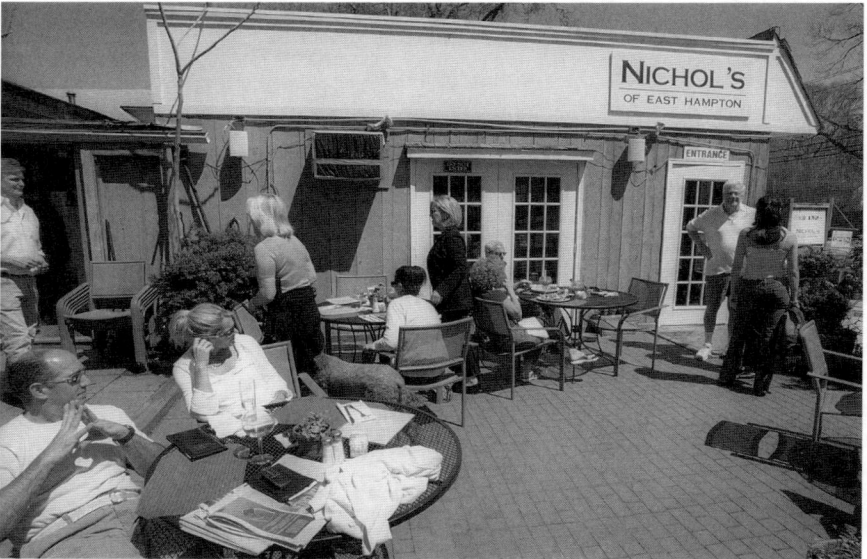

Our meal started with some interesting lightly fried bread rolls. The appetizers we didn't try included soup of the day ($5), baby back ribs ($8), a goat cheese and walnut salad ($10), and quesadillas ($13). Judging by the jumbo size of other dishes, a number of these would be large enough for an entree.

We did try a huge plateful of excellent mussels ($11) and two large crab cakes for $9 that came with two interesting sauces, one a mango-based salsa. The spinach salad with bits of crisp bacon and hard-boiled egg was nicely balanced and a perfect start to a meal. I think it just edged ahead of an excellent beetroot salad with blue cheese, artichoke hearts, mesclun, and tiny, oven-baked tomatoes.

We were off to a good start, but would the entrees disappoint? Certainly not — that $12 fish pie, which had big chunks of lobster in its creamy sauce in addition to scallops, white fish, peas, and corn, all topped with mashed potatoes, was delightful. The scallops, cooked scampi-style, equally so.

Expecting to see a filet mignon the size of a thumbnail, we were agreeably surprised to find that it was a fine, upstanding example of the genre, and beautifully cooked to boot. We agreed that the sauce it was served with was a little too sweet, but it really didn't need it anyway.

There was a lovely piece of salmon served with rice and a huge bowl of penne with fresh tomatoes and squash that set off no fireworks but was perfectly okay. About the only thing that left us cold was a dull selection of sliced squashes and peppers — but they looked pretty.

And the best was last — a wonderfully tart Key lime pie and an outstanding lemon cake, with a crisp, sugary crust and a light, soaked, baba-style middle. If you go, do leave some room for it.

At dinner at Nichol's the price is right, the food is good, the portions are generous, the service is excellent, and the setting is most attractive even though the music is a bit loud. I wish they would take reservations days ahead, but that was about the only complaint we had.

April 2003

NICK AND TONI'S

136 North Main Street

East Hampton

324-3550

Dinner seven days and Sunday brunch.

Nick and Toni's remains one of our most popular restaurants long after its tap dance in the spotlight as the in-place of the Hamptons. There is always a new hot spot, but if it is all buzz and no substance, by the end of the season it is as welcome as week-old haddock.

To remain a winner a restaurant has to have excellent food and service, of course, but Nick and Toni's has captured the elusive quality that translates not just to customer satisfaction but customer affection.

It has consistently good food that changes with the seasons, a slightly eccentric layout that actually adds to its charm, soft lighting and soft colors, an agreeable noise level, and the most enticing art in any restaurant on the East End. (The latter includes two insouciant stone dogs and the targets from an old shooting gallery that I would sell my grandmother to have.)

Between the bar and the wood-burning oven — which turns out great pizzas — is the first dining room, a casual area that sees a lot of traffic as customers trek to and from the main dining rooms at the back. That space is more peaceful, with a sound-absorbing carpet and generous space between tables.

The service is efficient and tactful, avoiding both intrusive bonhomie and napkin-snapping formality. Wines by the glass tend to be expensive, but there are a fair number of reasonably priced bottles. Menu prices are South Fork high end, with appetizers between $10 (green salad) and $14 (bay scallops and orecchiette) and entrees from $24 (roast chicken) to $42 for a rib-eye steak.

But... On Wednesday, Thursday, or Sunday evenings there is a whole range of first-rate pizzas for $16 or under and, until Memorial Day, there is a "Film and Food" offer that gets you a salad, a choice of entrees, and a movie ticket for $25.

One of our reviewing crew went for the latter, as good a bargain as you can find, and was completely happy with his Caesar salad, margherita pizza, and future free entry to "Starsky and Hutch."

We tried two lovely salads. One was farro and arugula mixed with raisins, pistachios, and mushrooms, very fresh and crunchy. The other was a superbly complementary mix of baby spinach, well-roasted red peppers, and duck confit with a lively blood orange vinaigrette.

An interesting dish of orecchiette, bay scallops, arugula, roasted cauliflower, and black truffles was really too big and would have been improved by chucking out half the orecchiette, which overwhelmed it.

One of the special appetizers of the day was a delicious little cheese and onion tart, with the onions cooked down to a perfect soft caramel color but not burned in the least. It came with a beautifully seasoned frisée salad.

Of my many visits to Nick and Toni's, this was the first occasion when any dishes were not up to par and, wouldn't you know it, the same person got them both. The first was a green salad that was too salty to eat, the second was an entree of tilapia, a nice firm-fleshed fish, which was almost without taste.

While we were waiting for our entrees the chef sent out a sample of a risotto made with wood-roasted porcini mushrooms. It was perfect, the dream that is lingering at the back of your mind whenever you order risotto, only to awaken to a plate of wet mush or enough oil to call a Hazmat team.

Another version of this wonderful risotto, without the mushrooms but with a hint of lemon, was served with the tuna, two perfect chunks of seared fish served over barely wilted spinach, to my mind the winning entree of the evening.

Both the halibut, surrounded by a cheery crowd of little red and yellow beets, chard, and whole cloves of garlic roasted to sweetness, and some beautifully sweet dorado, which came with chick peas and escarole, were also very good. We seem to have gone all out for fish this time, but we also tried a buttery lamb shank, a comforting cold-weather dish that will doubtless soon vanish from the menu as spring arrives.

We did not try it this time, but I always make a point of mentioning Nick and Toni's roast chicken in case anyone should say "Chicken? Boring." If it is still cooked the same way as it was before, it is a great dish.

I sometimes think that dessert should be served first, not at the end of the meal when you have already eaten too much.

On this occasion we got to try a good number of Nick and Toni's desserts. The talked-about dessert here is the $14 tartufo (sufficient for four) which is a sculpture of chocolate, pistachio, and caramel ice cream with various sauces. But, frankly, it is just ice cream, and ice cream is for fourth graders.

Try instead a panna cotta served with small slices of peeled blood orange that will make you think you have died and gone to heaven. Subtle in taste, exquisite in texture, and low in sugar, it is what you need at the end of a meal.

Equally good was the apple crostata, a perfect little basket of flaky pastry filled with aromatic apple slices, and a flourless chocolate cake with a fierce chocolate punch and a wonderful sauce made from cream cheese and espresso.

On second thought, perhaps the best way to end a meal would be the pastry chef's almond biscotti, served with a glass of vin santo to dip them in, or a sublime lemon sorbet (not for fourth graders) with a wisp of a meringue.

It is so good to see that Nick and Toni's has not lost its zest and enthusiasm over the years.

March 2004

THE PALM AT THE HUNTTING INN

94 Main Street

East Hampton

324-0411

Dinner seven days. Reservations for four or more.

Any good restaurant that endures for more than a couple of years develops a distinctive ambience, in part through the decor and the attitude of its staff and in part from the aura it picks up from its clientele — rich and restrained, maybe, or Downtown artysmarty, or harassed yuppies-with-young.

The atmosphere at the Palm on a packed-out Saturday evening over Easter weekend can be summed up by the three separate occasions that a group of waiters emerged from the kitchen, cake held aloft, and loudly serenaded some pink-cheeked diner with "Happy Birthday."

It's that kind of place — celebratory and high calorie and comfortingly old-fashioned.

As one of the decreasing number of shrines to rare red meat and jumbo lobsters, I suspect its jolly waiters must sometimes feel like the priests at the Temple of Apollo as the no-more-fun-and-games-for-you Christians started to outnumber the lions and push out the old religion.

Half of the appeal of the place lies in its low pressed-tin ceilings and comfortable banquettes with brass trimmings, like some Hell's Kitchen beanery from the 1920s. The waiters are old-style, too. They're both amazingly efficient and completely friendly, without any of that schmaltzy "my name is Sebastian and I will be taking care of you this evening" stuff.

The one thing that you have to know when dining at the Palm is that not only is it advisable to share dishes, because the portions are so large, but it is perfectly okay to do so. Of course you can do this at other places, too, but you run the risk of that masterly split second pause before the waiter replies, "Split the dish? Of course." A pause just long enough to make you feel cheap.

Once you know you can share, then the sight of steaks and chops all over $30 or a side order of creamed spinach for $8 won't give you a nasty shock. There were five of us dining on Saturday, three people shared a salad, two shared a $17 crabmeat cocktail, and three shared a 36-ounce New York strip steak for two.

Divided in two, that crabmeat cocktail still provided a generous helping — in fact it's hard to imagine one person eating the whole thing with the thought of a steak the size of a whale lying in their immediate dining future.

There are a number of other old warhorse appetizers like shrimp cocktail or Clams Casino and a big selection of self-explanatory salads. The one unidentified salad is Gigi salad for $12 which, as it is twice as much as the other salads, you might be tempted to ignore. Don't. It was more than big enough for three people to share and it was fabulous — tomato, green beans, sweet onion, frizzled bacon, and shrimp. The dressing was perfect and the taste and texture combination was like spring sunshine after the dreary winter of the mixed green salad.

The 36-ounce steak is a house specialty and priced at a daunting $65. But our three diners laid into it for first, second, and third helpings and there was still enough to take home a doggy bag for lunch for two the next day.

The Palm is famous for its side dishes, particularly the creamed spinach and some spectacular hash browns, though potatoes are served half a dozen different ways. In addition to the red meat dishes there are five veal dishes for around $21, three chicken dishes under $20, and a selection of seafood.

Lobster is a house specialty, and the Palm crab cakes (three large ones for $27) are excellent. But when it comes to fish, they seem a little out of their depth, so to speak. The fillet of sole was dry and overcooked and not so much dull tasting as unpleasant. Stick with the steak.

The Palm offers a decent selection of conventional desserts, of which the cheese cake was very good, and a large wine list, most rather high-priced. Do check the prices of the wines by the glass before you order. One of us ordered a glass of chianti, expecting it to be inexpensive, which turned out to be a stiff $10.50.

When the Palm is busy, which means every weekend and all through the summer, it can be very noisy. If you are lucky enough to have a choice, pick a quiet week night to step back into the past for a friendly, hearty, Currier & Ives evening.

April 2002

ROWDY HALL

10 Main Street

East Hampton

324-8555

Lunch and dinner seven days. No Reservations.

Rowdy Hall earned its name on Friday — it was packed with noisy diners at lunchtime and there were still people waiting for tables at nearly 3.

There was a large table of Whitmore's tree guys, parents arriving with babies so wrapped against the cold they looked like beach balls, and slews of out-of-towners. Was it the cold weather? New Year's conviviality? The East Hampton Cinema showing some decent movies for a change?

Or is it that Rowdy Hall has worked out a winning formula over the years and has the common sense not to change it?

The menu is small (a bit larger for dinner) but with a lot of variety. The portions are generous, and one dish is generally all you need, whether it is a main entree or just a soup or salad.

Most of the dishes have been on the menu for years, surviving even a rotation of chefs (the sturdy Arts and Crafts furniture would surely have been trampled to matchsticks if any changes had been made).

There is a French onion soup that would bring a stone to life and mussels in a white wine and shallot broth with a touch of cream that are not only good but *consistently* good. The Rowdy burger and fries are cooked the way the Almighty decreed. ("I have given thee the hamburger so thou shalt not be tempted to eat the fruit of the Tree of Life.")

The salads always have enough of a ratio of good stuff to healthy stuff to be completely satisfying. My favorite is endive, lettuce, Gorgonzola, and toasted walnuts, but the stout salad of fresh salmon, new red-skinned potatoes, onion, and black olives over mixed greens we tried on Friday was a delight.

The most expensive item on the lunch menu is fish and chips at $15. The cod is silky fresh and the batter, which is made with beer, is as light as tempura. The fish is served rolled up in newspa-

per in proper Cockney style and they even give you malt vinegar to put on your fries.

Be warned that you need a good appetite for lunch, or at least the opportunity to take a siesta later — the sandwich dishes in particular are dauntingly large. We tried a fine Reuben the size of a Honda Civic and, quite the best sandwich I've tasted for many a year, a Croque Monsieur that would have fed the whole East Hampton Highway Department.

Croque Monsieur is just a fancy name for a grilled ham and cheese sandwich, of course, but in this case the French sobriquet was warranted, because it was very special. And then there was a daily special of spicy black bean soup with chicken and chorizo that turned out to be excellent armor against the snowstorm that came the next day.

Nobody needed dessert, but our reviewing duties demanded that we try a couple. Two members of our team made an embarrassing spectacle of themselves over the warm chocolate cake with vanilla ice cream in a hard chocolate shell and more chocolate in the form of a powerful chocolate sauce.

I preferred an apple galette with an excellent crust, even though the apple filling was somewhat over-seasoned.

The restaurant was looking extremely festive, with glass tree ornaments hanging from the ceiling and lending a bit of color to the brown-on-brown decor. The bar was a surprise — at night it is rather dark, but in the daytime it is illuminated by panels of colored glass in brilliant yellows and blues.

The service was rather slow but, as mentioned before, the place was besieged with people. You would have thought it was August.

A movie and a bite at Rowdy Hall has become part of many people's lives in East Hampton and they like it just the way it is, even with all that fake Stickley.

Just leave the fish and chips the way they are, please.

January 2001

SAM'S RESTAURANT

36 Newtown Lane

East Hampton

324-5900

Dinner seven days.

Can a village lose its soul? One doesn't have to look much farther than Main Street, East Hampton, to see what happens when the quirky and the small are driven out. In the 1980s there was still a five-and-dime, "Pets Painted With Love," a liquor store, Whimseys, and Marley's.

Now the street has all the soul of boiled rutabaga.

But Newtown Lane, just around the corner, still has enough survivors of boutique botulism to attract people who live and work here — two hardware stores, Second Nature, Promised Land, Bucket's Deli. And Sam's.

Sam's, run by the grandson of the original Samuel Nasca, is best known for its pizza, but there is a whole menu of down-to-earth, old-school Italian dishes at reasonable prices. And takeout.

You can tell Sam's has been around a long time (since 1947) because it has a neon sign — Sam's bar and restaurant — which was put up long before the Board of Antimacassars and Finger Bowls decreed that signs must be tasteful to the point of invisibility.

Apart from a window box of flowers, the exterior is not very inviting. I think that is the way they want it — Sam's clientele already knows about Sam's.

Inside, the restaurant is small but very cozy. A narrow room with a bar and a row of tables does a dogleg into another long narrow room at the back.

The menu is hearty, but balanced by a big list of salads, small ones around $6, large ones around $10. The house salad is okay, but the tri-color salad of arugula, endive, and radicchio is more interesting and comes with a nicer dressing.

Pizzas start at $8 for a plain nine-inch and top out at $25.25 for a 16-inch Mediterranean Brava, with shrimp, crabmeat, pesto, and Gorgonzola cheese. Entrees go from $9.95 for pasta marinara to $18.95 for some of the seafood dishes.

A quick consensus of opinion around The East Hampton Star office revealed what we suspected: All had their favorite Sam's dish, they always order it, and it tends to be pizza. Pizza with mushrooms, pizza with goat cheese and sun-dried tomato, vegetarian pizza, and pizza with bacon, sausage, and hot peppers (whoa!) were among those mentioned.

So when we went there on Friday, while we didn't go so far as to have no pizza at all — we shared one as an appetizer, and very good it was too — we ventured out into new territory for our entrees.

Spaghetti with meatballs ($13.50) conjures up scary visions of gloppy pasta with bright red sauce and leaden golfballs of meat and comes right at the bottom of my culinary wish list. But Sam's could convert me, particularly with its meatballs, which are light and full of herbs yet completely different in composition from the Salisbury steak, which was a daily special ($15.50). Talk about comfort food!

I recommend the veal Milanese (17.95), which is simplicity itself: the veal lightly breaded and fried, with a blanket of fresh arugula, shavings of red onions, and chopped ripe tomatoes. The frutti di mare pasta ($18.95) was also no-nonsense, basically just carefully cooked linguine with shrimp, mussels, and clams. The Bolognese sauce at Sam's is rich, meaty, and brown, not red and acid, and the puttanesca sauce also gets raves.

The portions are very large — the veal Milanese could easily have fed two — and everyone at our table left toting a doggy bag.

For dessert there is apple crumble, tiramisu, cheesecake, and all the usual suspects, but we couldn't have eaten another mouthful.

Sam's. It's doing its part to keep East Hampton a village instead of just a place to shoot commercials for glossy magazines.

September 2002

THE 1770 HOUSE

143 Main Street
East Hampton
324-1770
Dinner seven days.

Perhaps the most memorable impression we carried away from a meal at the 1770 House last weekend was one of soothing relaxation.

The whole evening had been seductively easy from start to finish — cosseting service, little surprises, fine food, charming decor and presentation, a comfortable sound level — in just the way that a special meal in the Hamptons should be, but so often isn't.

The old house has been given an overhaul, but without removing any of its intimate and historical feel. Its small dining room, with old wood tables, soft lighting, and Oriental rugs, is elegant.

Judging by the battalions of vans and pickups that snarled traffic on Dayton Lane for months, the overhaul of the kitchen was much more radical. That means that the owners are surely in this for the long haul and must have carefully mapped out the demographics of their clientele. They are high-rollers.

I say that because, bucking the recent trend of lower prices we saw last year, the 1770 House is expensive. Perhaps that should not come as a surprise when one learns that the chef, Kevin Penner, was lured away from the Star Room, last season's priciest newcomer, though also the one with the best food.

So, before getting on to the good news — the food — here is the bad news. Wines are $9 to $15 a glass and there is nothing under $32 by the bottle, and precious little under $50, though the list is certainly impressive, with, for example, 10 different vintages of Chateau d'Yquem offered at pudding time.

Appetizers, nine of them, start at $11 for a mesclun salad, most are $16, with roasted foie gras being $23. (Don't even ask about the market price caviar.) Roast chicken is $26 and salmon is $28 but the other seven entrees are over $30, with grilled rib-eye steak topping out at $39.

Now that is out of the way, we can talk about nicer things, like the woven baskets, the immaculate presentation on elegant square white dishes, or the perfect *amuse bouche* of lobster salad on a slice of cucumber that was brought to each of us when we were seated — a single bite of summer perfection.

And talking about summer, if you try the 1770 House's Bellinis — champagne mixed with the fresh juice of white South Fork peaches — it will chase away the thought of Labor Day.

The dressings on all three salads we tried were exceptional, but the mesclun salad was a little overwhelmed by a fierce blue cheese. The heirloom tomato salad, on the other hand, was extraordinary — dream tomatoes, tomatoes that tasted the way they did when the world was young and the refrigerated truck uninvented.

Each constituent of the baby arugula salad was also perfect — the prosciutto, the wafers of pecorino cheese, the walnuts in the dressing, but there was so much of the good stuff in ratio to the arugula that it was more an antipasto than a salad.

And then there were two unusual appetizers: two curls of breaded and fried Dover sole with a caviar remoulade and a square of braised fresh pork belly with Asian greens, lobster mushrooms, and a sweet, spicy sauce — sounds a little weird but it was a knockout.

Someone else who had visited the restaurant said the striped bass was the best entree, and we had to agree. It was cooked very simply and served with a mixture of baby bok choy and spring onions over a sticky, almost sweet rice. There was a pile of green curry sauce, but it was a third wheel — the dish needed nothing more.

From the meat dishes, we chose the roast chicken, which, although it came with a lot of exciting accessories such as little puffy potatoes and a spicy corn relish, was a little dry. The person who ordered the $39 rib-eye likes his steak medium to well done. Had the steak been rare, maybe it would have been wonderful. As it was, it was on the chewy side. But, like our other quibbles, our complaints were minor and made partly because Mr. Penner seldom puts a foot wrong.

The lamb ($33) was superb, and a more generous helping than is customary. A wonderfully successful dish served with

Jerusalem artichokes, olives, and slow-baked tomatoes in a garlic and rosemary sauce.

Our last entree was the lobster risotto ($36). The risotto was perfectly cooked and intense in flavor, and there was lots, and I mean lots, of lobster piled on top of it. Our table was slightly in disagreement, some of us raving about it and others, well, me, actually, finding the flavors of saffron and fennel together to be a bit overwhelming.

While the presentation of all the dishes was beautiful, the desserts were breathtaking, each one accompanied by a contrasting sorbet or ice cream. It may be a cliché by now, but a great warm chocolate cake, with a melting middle, can't be beaten, cliché or not, and the 1770 House's is great.

The blueberry financier was, however, a blueberry muffin, pretty much. Not exciting. The delicate steamed lemon pudding was close to perfection but left a slightly bitter aftertaste.

The 1770 House is a place to put on your special occasion list. A place to go when you want to be pampered and spoiled and given delicate and imaginative dishes that arrive looking like Christmas presents.

August 2002

TURTLE CROSSING

221 Pantigo Road

East Hampton

324-7166

Dinner seven days. Brunch on Saturday and Sunday. Takeout. Seasonal.

It is like Goldilocks and the Three Bears. Restaurant reviewers get to visit some very expensive restaurants they would not dream of visiting if they were paying for themselves. They also have to go to a large number of places that they wouldn't dream of visiting if they didn't have to, inexpensive or not.

And then there are the restaurants that would have been their own choice.

Turtle Crossing is one of those places, where there is exciting Southwestern food, beautifully cooked and reasonably priced.

The décor is funky and no frills but comfortable enough, with various amusing signs such as "If you think you have a reservation, you're in the wrong place." Be warned that the portions are enormous.

It is almost impossible to resist beginning the meal with a margarita, which is not really such a good idea as it goes straight to your head, opens your appetite, and makes you eat more than is good for you.

This, I have decided, is my perfect Turtle Crossing dinner: two corn on the cob, rolled in Mexican cotija cheese and chili powder, and char-grilled ($6) followed by (a new entry on the menu since we were last there), chili-seared shrimp with guacamole, roasted corn and tomato relish, and a corn tortilla ($12).

But that's just my choice. Turtle Crossing is noted for its wood-smoked barbecue entrees — chicken, duck, ribs, brisket, pulled chicken, or pulled pork — which cost from $18 to $23.

Appetizers are $6 to $12, quesadillas are $12, burgers and sandwiches are $10, enormous wraps, big enough for three people, are $12 to $14, and other entrees are $10 to $18.

If you are going to order the basket of crispy artichokes for an appetizer, which you may well do because they are very good indeed, do not do it alone. You will need help to defeat this dish.

And the same applies to the pulled pork and mushroom quesadilla, which was the size of a pizza. But its size was deceiving because, unlike many quesadillas, the crisp tortilla shell was as light as a feather.

There was nothing deceiving about the size of the Hoisin barbecued duck wrap with spinach, pineapple salsa, mushrooms, rice, and black beans, however. If you had put wheels on it, it would have been a Hummer. It was delicious, but I had to give up after eating about a quarter and take it home in a doggie bag, where it will feed my family until Thanksgiving.

It would not have been right to visit Turtle Crossing without ordering ribs, which are as good as we remembered, and the cornbread is still the best on the South Fork.

The only dish that we were less than enthusiastic about was the beef enchilada which, with its hefty accompaniment of rice, beans, salsa, guacamole, and melted cheese, lacked the zip of the other dishes.

Now you would think that any four normal human beings would have eaten themselves to a standstill by this time, but we remembered that on a previous visit there had been an outstanding made-on-the-premises dessert.

So we drew a deep breath and ordered the peach cobbler, and discovered that it had not been a lucky chance the time before. This was an exemplary cobbler, with perfect crust, fresh peaches that had kept their firmness, and a fine pureed peach sauce. It seems a pity that most people have probably already given up before it is time for dessert — maybe they should leave a few bites of that quesadilla and plan ahead.

Turtle Crossing continues year after year to produce excellent Southwestern food at very reasonable prices. We were the last to leave, slipping away unnoticed by the staff, who were huddled in front of the television, mesmerized by the last inning of the second game of the World Series.

October 2003

MONTAUK

AFTER FISHING

467 East Lake Drive
Montauk
668-6535
Open daily from 7 a.m. for breakfast, lunch, and dinner.
No reservations. Seasonal

It was a stressful week — muggy heat, traffic, flash floods, fierce storms, and a power blackout — so to escape and relax we went to a restaurant that is just about as far as you can go on the South Fork without falling off.

After Fishing is on the second-floor deck of a building overlooking the Gone Fishing Marina on East Lake Drive in Montauk. On Sunday evening the skies had cleared, the humidity had dropped, and the temperature was perfect for eating outdoors.

You can't beat that view — Lake Montauk, rows and rows of sportfishing boats, and Star Island in the background. It was very quiet. The boats were moored and the fishermen had left, and the only movement was two black-capped night herons stalking the dock looking for prey. As night fell, mooring lights were reflected in the silken black water, its surface marred only by the popping ripples of surfacing fish.

First we felt relaxed, then we felt exhilarated, a state possibly helped by Bellinis made with local peaches. It was like going on vacation to a foreign country.

After Fishing opens really early in the morning to feed those hungry fishermen, then serves breakfast and lunch. The chef then takes a nap and is back on duty for dinner.

Our eyebrows rose when a plateful of the most heavenly home-made potato chips and a ramekin of bluefish paté arrived with the Bellinis — the evening was evidently not going to be all about deep-fried clam strips.

Having only been there for lunch, and that some years ago, I was unprepared for a menu that is both varied and ambitious, with words like duxelles, gremolata, and gaufrette popping up like little alien mushrooms.

There are many specials every night, including wine specials, and a good choice of inexpensive wines by the glass and bottle.

Presentation is as pretty as a picture. Prices are rather more mid-Hamptons than end-of-the-continent, with appetizers from $4.50 for a cup of chowder to $11.95 for a lobster martini cocktail and entrees from $19.95 for a vegetarian penne to $24.95 for filet mignon.

After Fishing is the current champion of the Best Clam Chowder in Montauk contest, having won the title in both 2002 and 2003. We all agreed that they deserve it; their chowder really is wonderful.

You can choose from among a number of salads, and such staples as mussels, clams on the half shell, lobster bisque, and Buffalo wings. We tried the fried lobster wontons with an orange dipping sauce ($9.25) which were crunchily good, and clam cakes, which had too much filler.

The house salad ($6.50) gets top marks for ingredients, which included the tiniest of string beans and some pungent olives, though the dressing was a little acidic.

One of our group was torn between ordering tuna or local cod as an entree. The tuna would have been a better choice, as the steamed cod ($19.50), served Japanese style in a basket with Asian greens, chard, and ginger was bland and overcooked and overwhelmed by the spicy peanut sauce. Also, I gather that it is not the time for local cod right now.

The swordfish ($22.95), however, was terrific. It was served with excellent mashed potatoes and baby asparagus, and came in a lemon, herb, and butter sauce with fat caperberries that it hardly needed.

After Fishing serves an ambitious seafood stew ($24.95), which includes clams, mussels, crab, shrimp, and an entire half a lobster. My only criticism would be that the flavor of the broth was too strong on the saffron and not strong enough on the essence of fish.

But not one word of criticism for the superlative lamb shank (which arrived with a single monarda blossom sticking out of the bone). The flavor was tremendous (it is the gremolata that counts — finely chopped garlic, lemon zest, and parsley added at the last minute) and imbued the tender meat, the carrots, tomatoes, and white beans that accompanied it.

The desserts we tried, a Key lime pie and a chocolate mousse-y, ganache-y little thing, were fine, though I wouldn't drive all the way to Montauk just for them.

But I would drive to Montauk, and beyond, for another visit to After Fishing.

The peace and serenity of the setting is a delight, the service is lovely, and the food is original and not too highly priced. And if the chef's reach occasionally exceeds his grasp, how much better to aim for the stars than churn out dull, predictable food that will surprise no one.

August 2003

BREAKWATER CAFE

Montauk Manor, Edgemere Road
Montauk
668-3949
Breakfast, lunch and dinner seven days.

The meal we had at the Breakwater Cafe (before it moved from the ground floor of a motel to the Montauk Manor) was the most elegantly prepared and the most beautifully cooked that I had had for a long time — and I've been batting a thousand recently in the places I have visited.

The prices were not the cheapest: $7 to $16 for appetizers and $15 to $28 for entrees, but neither were they the most expensive. The wines by the glass may seem a little high, but the bottle prices include many bargains.

The attention to detail was meticulous — excellent bread rolls, lovely olive oil, attentive service — and the presentation of the plates was downright art.

What made the green salad ($7) special, which was piled up like Richard Dreyfuss's mashed potatoes in "Close Encounters," was that it was made with tat soi, a peppery green, and mizuna, and a delicate, tomato-infused olive oil.

The Caesar salad ($9) was made with very finely sliced romaine lettuce and a good, pungent dressing. But if it's salad you want, then the winner was a confection of tiny warm beets served with braised greens, goat cheese, and toasted pecans. The sweetness of the beets contrasted with the slightly bitter greens, the sharp cheese with the unctuous nuts.

The crisp polenta fries were well received by our crew and the homemade ketchup they were served with was certainly enough to make you have second thoughts about that bright red stuff. But they made for a stodgy start to a meal, acting more as appetite-cutters than appetite-teasers.

Which brings me to what was, for me, the highlight of the meal, the softshell crab ($12). I know I have waxed a bit lyrical over these creatures a couple of times recently, but this one, this Breakwater Cafe paragon, was the ne plus ultra of soft shell crabs,

a ticket-to-the-Super-Bowl crab, a triple-crown crab, a Democrats-take-back-the-White-House crab. It was so crisp and light one could almost have blown it off its perch of spicy kimchee cabbage. A dab of sour cream, a circle of red pepper coulis — heaven.

The entrees kept up the high standard. As this was Montauk, they are mainly fish dishes, but you could have chosen a pork chop ($22), filet mignon ($28), or a giant burger ($15).

I think we were agreed that the Montauk swordfish ($21) was our favorite, but it was a close call between that and a pistachio nut-crusted salmon with chanterelles and mashed potatoes ($19) or halibut (caught on a dayboat trip) in a truffle broth with escarole and wild mushrooms, topped with a bird's nest of potato frizz ($22).

They had run out of the whole yellowtail snapper, stuffed with herbs and served with passion-fruit slaw and different sauces, but someone who tried it the night before said it was even better than the swordfish.

The tender free-range chicken ($19) was served with potato pancakes and grilled artichoke hearts that tasted almost fruity. The spring vegetable plate ($21) was much more exciting than the usual half-hearted nod that restaurants give to vegetarians, though the broccolini was a little too al dente.

Having been able to carry on a conversation all evening, we were in no hurry to leave and finished our meal with two desserts, a chocolate terrine with rum-soaked raisins, a dense oblong of intense flavor, and an orangewater-flavored crème brûlée. They were wonderful, the crème brûlée in particular. In fact, I swear it was the best....

Enough with the raving, already.

June 2003

DAVE'S GRILL

468 West Lake Drive

Montauk

668-9190

Dinner six days. Closed Wednesday.

May and October closed Monday through Wednesday. Seasonal.

Stop any 10 people on Main Street and ask them what they look for in an East End restaurant and it's a pretty safe bet that the answer would run along these lines: fresh local food, perfectly cooked but not too gussied-up, at reasonable prices, served in a friendly and relatively informal atmosphere.

But ask them how many times they find such culinary paragons and the answer wouldn't trip from the tongue so easily. But Dave's Grill in Montauk should certainly come to mind.

Having heard through the grapevine how good it was, we have had it on the reviewing list for a very long time, but as it is very popular and only takes same-day reservations, this weekend was the first time we were able to get a table.

The setting — right on the docks, with views of the Block Island Ferry docking and the Viking Fleet coming and going, not to mention a Labor Day full moon — is wonderful. The service is rapidissimo, with a feisty Montauk touch. ("I'm the head waitress, blonde and bitter.")

The arrival of the bread basket is often a reliable touchstone of what is to follow, and in this case the excellent bread augured well. It was served with olive oil poured into individual plates.

I'm curious — the last four restaurants visited have served olive oil instead of butter. Did some industry memo circulate saying, "At 4:30 p.m. on July 17 everyone will cut out the butter and give them nice healthy olive oil instead"? Not that I'm complaining.

We drank a Lindemann's Bin 65 chardonnay, a popular, inexpensive wine that served very well for the mainly seafood meal. On the menu, which changes periodically according to what is in season, most appetizers were $7.95 or $8.95, with soup at $5.95. There are a couple of more expensive items, such as coconut fried

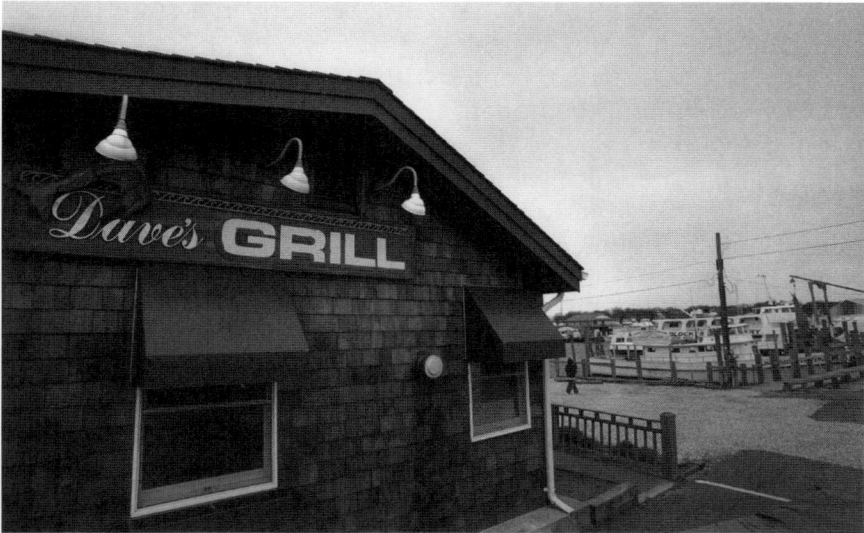

shrimp at $11.95 or a shellfish sampler at $14.95 with three different sauces.

On this evening, there was also a soup sampler, which gave us a chance to try the lobster bisque (superlative, with a strong lobster flavor and plenty of bits of lobster), New England clam chowder (also very good, with a nice herb seasoning), and the Manhattan clam chowder, which some of us found very good and others found on the dull side.

There is something fabulous called a tuna tempura sushi, which is like a tuna sushi roll but with unusual seasoning and rolled in a crunchy coating. The house salad was fresh and good.

We also tried one of the evening's specials: a Napoleon of breaded eggplant, herbed goat cheese, and smoked salmon. If it's available on the night you are there, grab it, because it was fabulous.

Entrees start at $17.95 for a vegetarian platter — a plain but well-cooked selection of grilled and steamed seasonal vegetables which are served with hummus and grilled pita. Vegetarians can also order the tomato, garlic, pepper, broccoli, and mozzarella penne dish without the sweet sausage it normally would contain.

The most expensive dish is Dave's cioppino at $26.95, but as this fish stew contained the best part of half a lobster in addition to fish, shrimp, mussels, calamari, and scallops in a superlatively rich, thick broth, it was worth every penny.

The sea bass, which comes with a light teriyaki glaze, could not have been improved upon. It came with spicy eggplant and a rice salad with snap peas. The grilled jumbo shrimp was almost as good, though the sauce could have had a bit more pep.

Seafood is definitely the thing to go for here — the tuna in a plum wine and ginger sauce was also excellent — though you could choose steak or pork chops if the fancy took you.

Dave's didn't fail when it came to desserts. The sorbet of the day was a delicate mango and there was a bread pudding made with rum that was light, warm, moist, and really deserved some grander name.

The crème brûlée was superb (as a mark of the service, its recipient was asked if she would like the sugar topping a little browner, and when she said yes, it was whipped back to the kitchen and returned a couple of minutes later with more of a Montauk suntan).

About the only criticism of our meal was that the patio dining area is rather noisy — so ask for an inside table if this is your particular bugbear. Otherwise, it is a relief and a delight to bring out that seldom-used metaphorical blue ribbon and pin it to Dave's menu.

September 2000

THE DOCK

I Town Road at Town Docks
Montauk
668-9778
Lunch and dinner seven days April I to Thanksgiving. Seasonal.
No reservations. No credit cards.

If you're the serious type looking for a serious establishment where you can enjoy serious food, the Dock may not be your cup of chowder. But if you have a taste for no-nonsense surf and turf and can appreciate the tongue-in-cheek sarcasm intended by such things as the "No Locals" sign above the front door or the "Do Not Enter" on the plate glass mirror by the bathrooms, then the Dock just might turn out to be your favorite restaurant.

At the edge of the commercial docks in Montauk Harbor, the saloon-style eatery boasts dark wood walls and floors, dim lighting, and a decor of wild memorabilia that tends toward the macabre. It has all the appeal of the ideal neighborhood bar and grill, but with better food and a little twist of something else.

Despite signs to deter screaming children and any form of complaining, the Dock's low prices and simple sandwich offerings, even at dinner, make it one of the last great places for a meal out with the kids. The very reasonable lunch and dinner menu tops out with entrees at $18 but also includes a tasty tuna melt made with a real tuna steak on an English muffin for $9, and burgers on muffins for $5.50 (a side of fries is $3).

If they are not scared off first, youngsters will no doubt get as much of a kick out of the boar, deer, and moose heads mounted around the dining room as most adults do. Should you need a conversation starter, there is something wacky in every corner of this small place, which is at least half of what makes it so great.

A painting of two boxers trading punches and another of Eisenhower hang over the bar. Taxidermy ducks fly by above it. There are funky signs and amusing photographs everywhere, the skull of a bull, a whale rib, and a sign that says "Pay Or Die."

A perfect snack or light meal at the Dock would include mussels bathed in a lip-smacking garlic, wine, and herb broth ($9), a basket of bread, a side of thin homemade fries, and a pint of beer. This combination has been enough to lure me to the Dock at least twice a month, and when it is closed for the season, I count the days.

The menu offers simple fare like fish and chips, burgers, fresh fish sandwiches, nachos, fried soft shell crabs, and linguine with clam sauce, while the specials board fills in with more substantial choices.

Though it's right on the docks and fish seems de rigueur, my preference where the specials are concerned tends toward turf rather than surf. One frequent special not to be missed is the mouthwatering grilled sirloin steak served with French fries and peppery spinach for $18. Delicious. Tops, too, are the tender marinated pork chops with still-crunchy grilled asparagus and piquant garlic mashed potatoes.

On the other hand, a scallop bisque, the soup of the day on a recent visit, was thick and good but not exciting. Also lackluster, though cooked just right, was an entree of broiled scallops with corn on the cob. The blackened mako special, in a spicy rub with mashed potatoes and veggies, was more impressive, but nothing beat the steak.

On the regular menu, a medium-sized bowl of steamed Little Necks ($11) comes in a broth just as worthy of bread-dunking as the mussel broth is.

If you expect a hearty hunk of bacon on your Clams Casino, you could be disappointed at the Dock. Here it means tasty clams but just a hint of bacon and instead a sort of herb butter-chopped red pepper combo. The nachos, however, are sure to please. Smothered in cheese, beans, sour cream, jalapenos, and salsa, they are, at just $9, a meal unto themselves.

As for the main menu entrees, I've always been partial, when the mood strikes, to the basic fish and chips. The soft shell crabs ($18), recommended by a friend, did not measure up. We loved the coleslaw and fries, but were bored with the crabs themselves, which were covered in an average breading without much flavor. Pump up the volume, we wanted to say.

Over-ordering at the Dock is almost an inevitability. So dessert, which is listed on the specials board and usually delicious, must often be shared. We split a slice of Key lime pie with a hearty

dollop of fresh vanilla whipped cream. It was not the Key lime pie a Southerner might know, but with a crispy graham cracker crust and zesty not-too-sweet filling it was delicious.

The Dock does not take reservations (or credit cards), so expect a 20 to 45-minute wait on a Friday or Saturday night. Some people belly up to the wooden bar, which runs half the length of the restaurant, for Guinness, Bass, Bud, or Bud Light on tap; others use the wait as a chance to wander the Gosman's complex or check out the fishing boats docked nearby. Whatever you decide to do, remember: Bring cash and no whining.

August 2003

EAST BY NORTHEAST

51 South Edgemere Street

Montauk

668-2872

Dinner seven days. No reservations.

There was something in the air at East by Northeast, a restaurant with an Asian touch on the very edge of Fort Pond in Montauk, and you could feel it the minute you walked in the door.

It wasn't an eating-out-at-a-restaurant buzz, it was a party buzz, the sound of people not only enjoying their food but having an inordinately good time. And it didn't take long to find out why.

East by Northeast was opened by the owners of the Harvest, a restaurant that has been consistently good and consistently popular since it opened. They know what they are doing. The chef is Anthony Sylvestri, formerly of Pacific East; the dessert chef, Derrick Goeltz.

The restaurant, which used to be Sunset Point and before that the Windjammer, had a complete facelift. The garish carpet has been replaced by glowing wood and inlays of tile and pebbles, the aqua Naugahyde chairs have gone and now there are tables with acid-etched copper centers. There are natural stone walls, a delightful bar, a glassed-in wine cellar, and, of course, the wonderful view.

One thing the renovation didn't cover was windows that open. Maybe that will happen in the future, because a future is what this restaurant is going to have.

As at the Harvest, the food is described as "family style," meaning it is a good idea to share things. We were seven. We ordered five small plates (between $8 and $18) to start and five large plates to follow (between $18 and $48, for a two-pound lobster) and it was more than enough. In fact, four of each would have been fine.

So, as far as prices go, it can be inexpensive or expensive. For two people you could share the indescribably good shredded chicken salad with napa cabbage, crisp wontons, and chili-lime vinaigrette ($12) and then share a big bowl of chicken or shrimp

Pad Thai noodles ($18) and your meal will have cost you $15 each.

Or you could greedily hog a tempura lobster roll and a sirloin steak yourself and spend $53.

The wine list is a little puzzling. Four reds by the glass at $7 or $8, but none of them sold by the bottle, and a list of reds by the bottle that is rather small and somewhat expensive. The whites have a wider choice and are more economical. But since the restaurant has been open only a couple of weeks, I suspect the wine list is a work in progress. The hot sake had run out the evening we were there and the cold sake is no substitute.

Service: Faultless.

Okay, enough of the chat. Let's get down to the food.

One of the reasons for the party atmosphere is that sharing food makes a meal very sociable, particularly when a couple of dishes on the menu turn sharing into performance art.

With shabu-shabu ($28), a pretty teapot of boiling mushroom broth arrives with its own tiny stove and a platter of raw seafood — tuna, scallops, salmon, shrimp — and various dipping sauces. You then cook the seafood yourself, ending up by pouring the delicious broth into tiny pottery beakers.

It is the same idea with the Japanese Hot Rock ($22), but here you cook slices of filet mignon and mushrooms on a baking hot rock before dipping them into a sweet soy sauce. I'm hard put to say which I liked best, as both were so good.

But that was at the "large plate" stage; before that there were all these terrific appetizers. In a poll of seven, the winner by a narrow margin was the meltingly tender Peking duck, squeezed inside featherlight tacos with a wonderful avocado salsa. So-o-o-o good. (At $12, big enough for an entree for one.)

Winner for best sauce was the mango, cashew, and hot chili around the seared sea scallops. For $11 you get a selection of beef and chicken sates with cucumber salad and a peanut sauce. The pork and shrimp spring rolls, while slightly less impressive than the other dishes, were nonetheless very good.

The caramelized halibut, a large plate at $26, was beautifully cooked, but was unusual in that what came with it, vegetables and noodles in a tamarind orange broth, was as good as the fish. The pepper-crusted tuna was wonderful, at $30 quite enough for two, with its accompanying passion fruit shrimp salsa and snow pea shoots.

The only dish that was less than stellar was the Pad Thai, whose noodles tended toward the gluey rather than the bouncy, but that was only in comparison with the excellence of the other dishes.

Although we were completely full, there was no way we were going to miss the desserts, having had advance word that they were very special. If you can face only one, make it the banana spring rolls with two pots of dipping sauce, one caramel, one chocolate.

The others we tried were almost as good: an intense, dense chocolate truffle cake with honey yogurt ice cream and a row of raspberries, each one in a little pool of raspberry coulis. A coconut tapioca pudding with passion fruit syrup and meringue fingers which arrives with a little spoon-shaped cookie balanced on a scoop of coconut ice cream. Peanut butter parfait, glistening with chocolate glaze and topped with a crackle of sesame brittle.

East by Northeast has got it all: unusual and excellently cooked food, a great water view, exquisite presentation, a friendly atmosphere in an elegant setting. No wonder everyone was having such a good time.

August 2002

GOSMAN'S DOCK

500 West Lake Drive

Montauk

668-5330

Lunch and dinner seven days. Seasonal. No reservations.

The East End has restaurants that are grandly gourmet or interestingly ethnic or just cheap and funky. From marinated octopus to deep-fried ostrich, somewhere there's a joint that will serve it to you. And then there's Gosman's.

When your mother's in town, or that couple you met in Bolivia suddenly turn up on your doorstep, where do you take them? Gosman's, of course. I'm not saying the food is better than anywhere else, just that Gosman's is an East Hampton institution.

All winter long, if you've been eating out at all, it's been at a cozy local hangout with a fireplace — not too far to drive on a dark night. But when the shad blooms and the days get longer, the urge comes to take the road east to the end of the island to watch the fishing boats coming in — and eat at the same time.

It's safe to say that there's no other restaurant on the South Fork with a view quite like this, with boats batting to and fro only feet away and big hungry seagulls perched like vultures waiting for ill-guarded French fries.

On a recent Sunday (even at 3 p.m. the place as busy) we stopped at Gosman's with a particularly deadly reviewing weapon: badly behaved 2-year-olds. No one flinched, thrown forks and calamari rings were retrieved with grace, and extra napkins were provided without request (though I suspect that the smile on our waiter's face was pretty forced by the end of the meal.)

Those calamari, one of the ubiquitous appetizers we tried, were very good and the crab cakes, while not in the Nobel prize category, were a great deal at $6.95. The charred tuna sashimi is a treat.

As Gosman's specializes in seafood, you can always get clams, oysters, shrimp, scallops, steamers, bisques, and chowders, not to mention lobsters, which just walk up the beach and in the kitchen and are very much in demand.

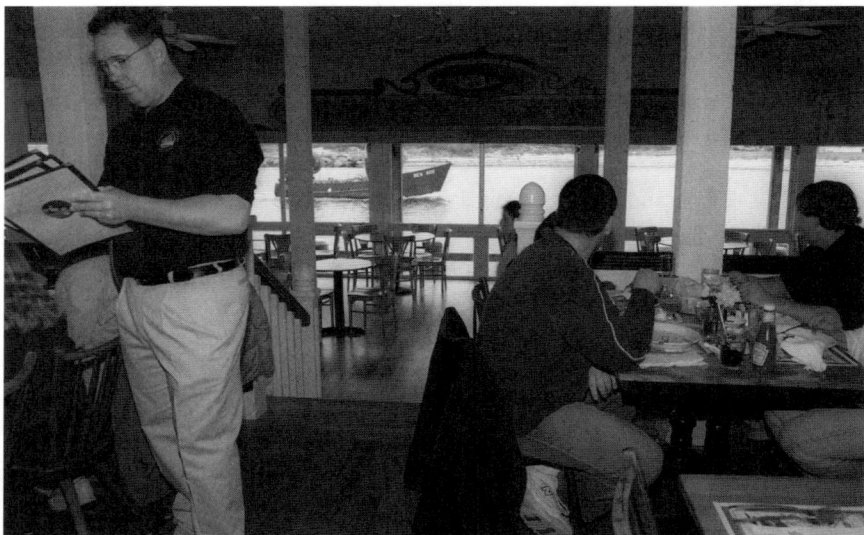

The choice of fish for entrees includes tuna, flounder, swordfish, fluke, and whatever fish comes in on the boats each morning. On this day one of the choices was cod, which was served in blackened Cajun style and was as fresh and luminous as a daisy.

But the sea bass, which came with a spicy, peppy sauce of diced peppers, scallions, corn, and herbs, was a piscatorial masterpiece of the kind that could have you renouncing red meat forever without a second thought.

Having said that, we did feel obliged to try something that wasn't seafood. And sure enough, the huge sirloin steak, nicely cooked but with too much fat and gristle left on its edges, did seem very meaty and indelicate when compared to the fish.

The children would have eaten more of their platter of breaded flounder fillets if they hadn't discovered that Gosman's salad smothered with blue cheese dressing was a far cry from the healthy-looking stuff they get at home.

We tried a couple of desserts — a strawberry-rhubarb pie and a chocolate-pecan pie — and were underwhelmed. As with the steak, we'd say stick to the fish.

There are good reasons why Gosman's is popular, which brings us to the only real caveat about the place — it's almost too popular. Since they don't take reservations, this means that there is often a long wait for a table, so don't go there if you're in a hurry.

Plan to sit in the sun on the terrace, watch the boats, and have a drink while you wait — the time will pass in a flash.

Gosman's certainly doesn't need a review to let people know it's there, perched on wooden pilings in the channel where Lake Montauk breaks through to the sea. Everybody knows that, just as everybody, sooner or later, says, "Let's go to Gosman's today."

May 2000

THE HARVEST

11 South Emery Street

Montauk

668-5574

Dinner seven days. Seasonal.

Family-style restaurant? The picture that comes to mind is one of harassed parents knocking back martinis and gazing glassy-eyed at a row of small children elbow deep in ketchup.

The Harvest certainly isn't like that. All family-style means here is that the portions of its excellent food dictate that they be shared by two. This means that the prices, which at first glance seem high — $14 to $24 for appetizers and $15 to $42 for entrees — are actually very reasonable.

It also means there is a party atmosphere to the meal. You have, say, six people passing dishes around the table, trying a bit of this and a bit of that, with everyone talking at once. It's like eating in a Chinese restaurant.

It is certainly more sociable than sitting alone behind your all-to-yourself entree, which turns out to be the culinary lemon of the evening, and wishing you could dig into your neighbor's sizzling steak, which looks so much better.

So the Harvest has a good atmosphere, food that has remained consistently good for years, and a bright, uncluttered space with an interesting layout.

But it also has a deck, and a dock, and Fort Pond — a little sea mist creeping across the water, kayakers slipping through the water as the sun sets, a mill pond calm with ducks, heads down, or the nighttime reflection of a hundred distant lights.

A water view — one of the best things about eating out in the Hamptons. The devil recently had to call a moratorium on soul deals with restaurateurs because they all asked for the same thing and he had no water views left except at the Gowanus Canal.

Well, enough of that. What about the food? There is a choice of about 10 appetizers, including mussels, tabbouleh salad, seafood bruschetta, and grilled asparagus, pizzas, pastas, salads, and half a dozen meat and fish dishes.

The calamari salad ($19) is big enough for three and has a wonderful frisée salad liberally studded with light, crisp, battered calamari. It is one of the dishes that the Harvest is known for. Equally good was a salad of grilled portobello mushroom with crisp deep-fried patties of goat cheese and mixed greens.

Although it is listed as a side dish, the Harvest's spinach with mushrooms and shallots is so special that we ordered it as an appetizer. The onions and shallots are gently cooked to slightly caramelized softness and the spinach was barely introduced to the pan before being whipped out onto the plate. The elusive, nutty flavor of the dressing ties it all together.

For entrees we tried one of the daily specials, grilled duck with crisp skin and the breast slightly rare, served with wild rice and delicious apricot chutney. There was enough of the porter-house steak with a green peppercorn sauce to ensure all six of us had some, and the same was true of the red snapper, the size of a fisherman's lie, which came with a big tangle of julienned vegetables and a tangy sauce. Add to that a side order of garlic mashed potatoes and you had a tableful of very happy diners.

An $18 dessert plate (that's $3 a head) came with an excellent flourless chocolate cake, featherlight tiramisu, perfectly raisined bread pudding, and even so was almost too much for us to finish.

Although we did not try them this time, both pastas and pizzas are recommended, and if the thought of paying $8 for a side order is a bummer, remember that the Harvest's are very big and very good.

If you have a restaurant that is consistently popular and hard to get into during the season, there is a good reason for it. The one thing to mention is that it is best to go with at least four people; a couple will find themselves sharing just one dish or taking a lot of food home.

March 2004

IL MARE

Montauk Yacht Club, 32 Star Island Road
Montauk
668-3100
Dinner seven days. Seasonal.

The restaurant at the Montauk Yacht Club, which you reach by crossing the causeway to Star Island in the middle of Lake Montauk, is now called Il Mare.

The place is somewhat over-flunkied for my taste. Between the door and the entrance to the restaurant we were welcomed by four different people. But that would not be a criticism for some.

The restaurant's biggest plus is its fabulous view across Lake Montauk. If you time it to coincide with the most spectacular lightning storm we have had on the East End in a year, as we did on Friday, so much the better. The lightning over the lake and the rain crashing on the skylights overhead added zest to the meal. And when the weather is warm there are tables outside, which is unbeatable.

The biggest minus is the restaurant's anonymous hotel convention center atmosphere (and, indeed, Salomon Smith Barney was having a wingding nearby as we ate). There is not so much of a hint, in the staff or the ambience, of the feisty hamlet next door — and most people who come to Montauk want to find Montauk, not Central Nowhere.

After we had protested about being seated at a table for eight when there were only five of us and had been moved to a place where we were able to communicate better with one another, the meal got off to a good start with an *amuse bouche* of black olive tapenade on toast, a good selection of bread and rolls served with herbed olive oil, and a reasonably priced Chianti.

Appetizers start at $5.75 for a Tuscan bean soup, rise to $14 for lobster spring rolls, and include several unusual items, including baby lamb chops and a hot seafood antipasto.

The carpaccio of octopus sounded interesting and looked spectacular in its flower-like arrangement of paper-thin slices, but the slices were so thin they were gone in two mouthfuls, their slight flavor evanescing on the tongue like foam: "Did I eat that, or did I just imagine it?"

The julienned salad on which the octopus rested, well tossed with a lemony basil dressing, was very good, however. As was the special house salad, which is topped with roasted peppers, Gorgonzola cheese, and macadamia nuts.

For $8 you get a lively fritto misto of fried squid and scungilli with grilled vegetables, oily and tasty and satisfying. It must be said that the waitstaff didn't seem to be entirely knowledgeable about what they were serving because the daily special of Prince Edward Island clams on the half shell turned out to be oysters.

It being Montauk, we went all out for seafood, with perhaps the most exciting dish being a canneloni of three different fish served with a wonderful lobster sauce. It was light and the flavors complemented one another rather than drowning one another out.

The grilled tuna ($24), which came with grilled polenta and a terrific roasted red pepper coulis, was also very good. Monkfish ($22), the plain Jane of the fish world unless you do something to it, came with cabbage, leeks, and potatoes and was very dull. A better bet was the garlic shrimp pomodoro ($24), a hip-hoppy melange of hefty shrimp in a sauce of diced tomatoes, basil, garlic, and white wine.

But in the end, the guest who went for the most conventional dish, chicken, was the surprise winner. The whole poussin was stuffed with sweet sausage and sundried tomatoes and coated in a honey and coriander sauce. It proved that chicken can compete if you treat it right.

As we could not make up our minds, we were talked into the dessert platter, at $25 almost too much for five people to manage. It would have sent Wayne Thiebaud into paroxysms of artistic enthusiasm with its mixture of pastel colors and pretty presentation. First there was a collection of semi-freddo ice creams, then there was a really wonderful cheesecake, little warm cakes of chocolate, and, most interesting of all, a basil mousse.

The prettiest dessert was a wafer basket filled with a ricotta cheese concoction and decorated with raspberries (regretfully it tasted like chicken salad) and there was also something red and strange that could have been made from tomatoes.

To sum up: Il Mare is comfortable and there is an agreeable amount of space between tables. The carpet, while not a thing of beauty, ensures that the acoustics are good. The view is great and the chance of eating outdoors even more so. The food is imaginative, well flavored, and good, though it reminded me a little of a woman with just a touch too much cleavage and one gold chain too many.

June 2002

OYSTER POND

4 South Elmwood Avenue
Montauk
668-4200
Dinner seven days. Lunch Friday, Saturday, and Sunday.

I know someone who drives to Montauk to eat at Oyster Pond just for the "chocolate bag" dessert — a solid shell of chocolate shaped like a bag and filled with cream, ice cream, chocolate sauce, and sauteed banana.

But, for most of us, it takes more than dessert to lure us to a restaurant. Luckily, the rest of Oyster Pond's bill of fare is exciting enough to reel in diners like bluefish in fall. Add to that warm and friendly service and extremely pretty surroundings, and you have a winning combination.

We had made a reservation for four, and when we arrived with an extra guest it didn't put the waitstaff out at all. It was to our advantage, in fact, as we were seated on the screened porch, a warm room with a lovely collection of etchings and a raftered ceiling, where the only hint of the fierce wind blowing outside was the slight bellying of the heavy window plastic, which seemed appropriately nautical.

The wines by the glass are well chosen and reasonable, though for my money I find the wine list too expensive and, in that it is 95 percent Californian, rather narrow.

Appetizers range from $6 for soup to $11 for crab cakes, but there is also the pu pu platter, $14 for one person or $20 for two, which gets you a selection of four different items.

They include grilled oysters, which are transformed into some other exotic animal by the addition of roasted garlic, red pepper and bacon, and smoked tomato aioli. Then there is a crunchy spring roll with lemon thyme syrup that for once really is like spring and not the sad, damp autumn of most spring rolls. The honey-sesame glazed tempura shrimp may be the best tempura on the East End.

Almost equally good was the Oyster Pond salad, which had a wonderful spicy, peanutty Oriental vinaigrette. In addition to chopped Romaine hearts and thinly sliced sweet onions, it had

caramelized pecans and, maybe one ingredient too many, fresh orange slices.

Since it was such a knockout, my recommendation would be to start with a salad and have a pu pu platter, small or big, to follow.

The final item was a spicy sushi tuna roll, which was slightly less exciting than the other ingredients but was accompanied by a divine sweet-and-sour cucumber salad.

Entrees run from $19 to $24, and there is also a choice among six pizzas, none more expensive than $14.

On Friday there was a special clambake available. For $19, a bowl of excellent New England clam chowder with a strong herby kick was followed by a big heap of clams, mussels, sweet corn, and a fresh lobster. Good value.

Another special of the day was halibut, served with shiitake mushrooms in a broth that was livened up with ginger, over brown rice and smothered in a pile of julienned vegetables. Simple and very good.

The monkfish dish was fun. The fish was cut into squares, dusted with macadamia nuts, roasted, and served with garlic mashed potatoes and sauteed spinach. The potatoes and spinach were perfection, to the point that they overshadowed the fish. And why not? There's no rule to say that vegetables can't be the stars of the show occasionally.

The salmon dish was also fun, but here the idea of wrapping small pieces of it in nori seaweed and roasting it was rather less successful, because it came out a little dry and needed the terrific red onion chutney that came with it. While the brown rice that accompanied it was perfectly okay, everyone hankered for those garlic mashed potatoes.

Beware the seafood castellane — it's huge. A serving platter of lobster, shrimp, clams, and mussels over penne, its marinara sauce was rescued from the pedestrian by a good hot chili kick. You won't need an appetizer before this and you certainly won't be able to manage the chocolate bag afterward.

Which takes us to dessert, where we eschewed the chocolate bag for two new desserts, which did not serve us as well. I have a feeling the apple crisp crumble is normally very good but someone had goofed with the baking time and it came out raw. The pumpkin parfait sounded interesting, but wasn't.

The last time we ate at Oyster Pond there seemed to be one ingredient too many in each dish. This has been corrected, without losing the lively and imaginative flair of the menu.

May 2002

SHAGWONG RESTAURANT

774 Main Street

Montauk

668-3050

Lunch and dinner seven days.

The Shagwong in Montauk is celebrating its 30th year in business. If the crowds there on Saturday night are anything to go by, it'll probably make it through another 30 or, who knows, maybe even as long as it takes to decide the presidential election.

It's a down-to-earth place where the diner's appetite is honed for dinner by the rigorous workout it takes to get through the crowded bar and attain the dining room.

On a less busy night, diners can see a wonderful collection of photos of old Montauk on the walls and discuss them in muted voices. Not so on a Saturday. The noise level is intense because, in contrast to many a more upscale establishment, it really seems as if everyone is *having a good time.*

There was a table in the window with five brawny, bearded guys in caps straight off a fishing boat (or from the set of "A Perfect Storm"). There were couples with small children, family groups, and at least two girls-night-out tables. It's really nice to hear so much laughter.

Shagwong's prices are reasonable. There's a choice of six wines by the glass — including a Chilean merlot, a Cotes-du-Rhone, and a Forest Glen cabernet sauvignon — that cost $5 or $6.

All the entrees, $15 to $24, come with a choice of appetizer. À la carte appetizers range between $3.75 for clam chowder to $7.50 for mussels or calamari (both big enough dishes to serve as an entree).

A good impression is made at the very start of the meal because the restaurant takes the trouble to serve a selection of good breads and offers a little pot of homemade hummus as well as butter to eat with them.

We tried a finely seasoned black bean soup just made for a chilly fall evening, a good fresh salad with the usual green and red

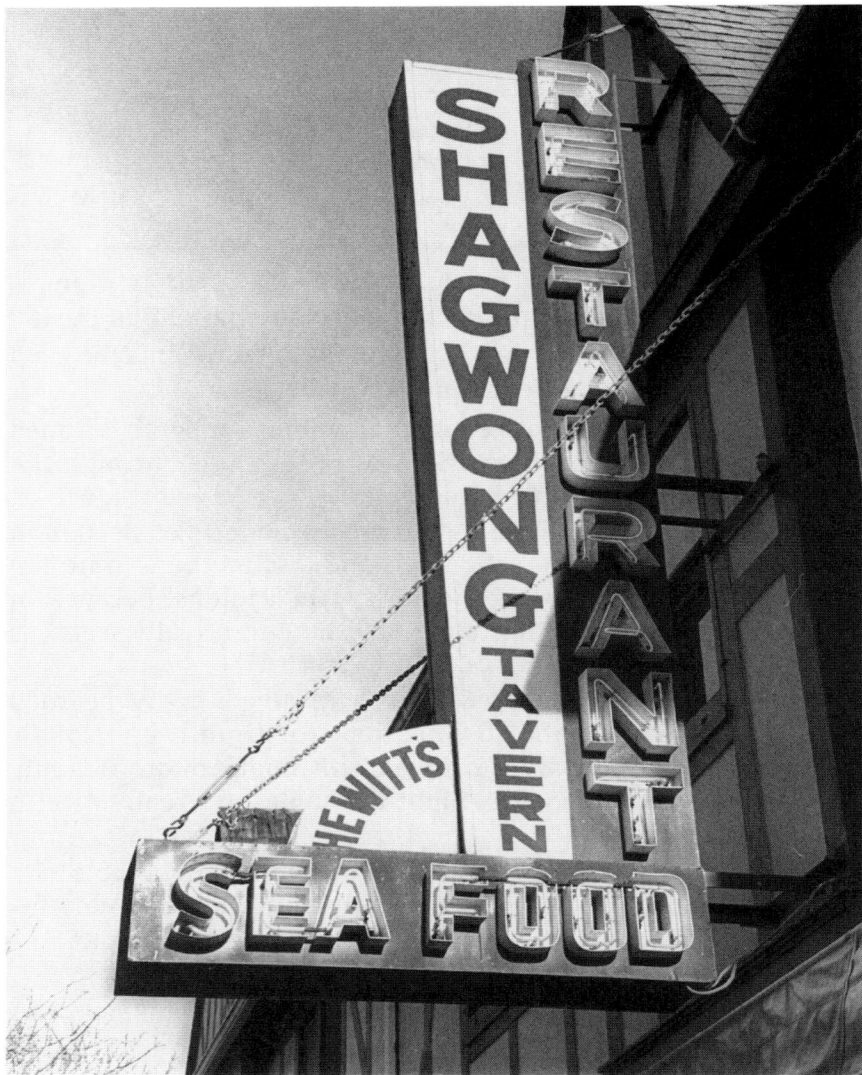

bits, and some homely codfish cakes with a nice roasted tomato sauce.

The mussels were excellent and, as I mentioned, a generous serving. The calamari, on the other hand, were rather disappointing, with an uninspired breadcrumb coating and a sauce that could be improved upon.

When eating out in Montauk, seafood is always a safe bet, of course, and the perfectly cooked lobster chosen by one of our party was maybe the entree of the night. At $20 it was also reasonably priced.

Sauteed sea scallops, served with mixed root vegetables and really good spinach, were fine, if not very exciting. The "Angry Soft Shell Crabs" were exciting, in that they had a fierce, overpowering sauce, but the crabs themselves were rather mushy. And I have to say, in an undertone maybe, that on this occasion the striped bass, that silvery icon of fine East End fish, was overcooked.

A happier choice was the filet mignon, marinated and very tender, and, although we didn't try it this time, the rack of lamb can be outstanding.

One thing to note: When you are offered a multiple choice of potatoes, go for the mashed, because they are exceptionally good. The menu used to specify that they were Zebrowski's Bridgehampton potatoes, but it no longer does. What happened to Zebrowski's farm? Covered in million-dollar starter castles, probably.

Both desserts we tried, an apple tart and a raspberry almond torte, were really wonderful.

Every seat was taken in the restaurant and the bar looked as if it was competing for the "entire population of a village crammed in one room" Guinness record, but the service was perfect. After a slightly sluggish start suddenly there was a waiter at one's elbow the minute a glass was empty. Perfect? — It was Alain Ducasse; it was Le Bernadin.

Not to suggest that Shagwong's service is anything less than excellent, but I figure the reviewer was sussed.

November 2002

TRAIL'S END

Edgemere Road

Montauk

668-2133

Dinner seven days. Seasonal.

Trail's End is the oldest restaurant in Montauk and one of the oldest on the East End. Its building, not much larger than a garden shed, once stood on the bay where the old Montauk fishing village was before the Hurricane of 1938. It survived the storm, which left Montauk an island for three days, and was then moved to its present location.

It was under one management for 57 years until bought by the present owners in 1983.

The odds are that you haven't been there unless you live in Montauk — much of its facade is taken up by a noxious neon sign that makes people exchange a horrified glance and drive straight past.

Which is a pity, because Trail's End, just after the Circle on the way to the docks, is good value, serves very good food, and is as cute as a button inside. Indeed, if you are very tall, you might bump your head on the ceiling. The decoration will put you in mind of a dollhouse. It's the sort of place where you can't fail to relax. There is music of a gently corny type (the soundtrack from "Sleepless in Seattle" the other night), but it is not intrusive.

The wine list is sensible, with only two bottles over $30, and there is a surprisingly large selection of wines by the glass, including champagne. The service is fast and efficient with just enough joshing to let you know this is Montauk and not East Hampton.

The list of daily specials is extensive, and there is a bargain $13.95 early bird prix fixe. Appetizers range from $3.95 for a cup of soup to $8.95 for mussels; entrees from $8.95 for hamburger and fries to $21.95 for steak.

I have to confess we were not expecting much, and the sight of Buffalo wings and mozzarella sticks on the menu confirmed our prejudices. But then excellent bread rolls arrived, followed by a really good lobster bisque (I didn't find much lobster, but the fla-

vor was first-rate), and light and tender deep-fried bites of chicken breast. We also tried some pleasant stuffed clams and a Caesar salad, though the latter needed a blood transfusion, as it tasted of little more than wet lettuce.

At $19.95, the roast duck (half a large one) with Grand Marnier sauce is highly recommended. The sauce wasn't brilliant but as it was served in a separate sauce boat it didn't interfere with the main business: juicy duck with crisp skin and great flavor and nice herb stuffing.

It was only outdone by some exemplary lamb chops ($21.95), one of the daily specials, though an unusually tender and moist pork chop threatened to catch them in a photo finish. As it is a small place, and as prices are reasonable, you wouldn't expect different vegetables with each dish. The vegetable "du jour," we were told, was carrots. This is a widely recognized code word for large chunks of orange matter that you immediately push to one side of the plate and ignore, so it was an eye-opener to find that they were really fresh, perfectly cooked, and buttery sweet, as was the broccoli that also turned up. A good sign, that.

The fish in the fish and chips ($14.95) was breaded flounder, perfectly nice but a little dull, a complaint that couldn't be made about the Southern fried chicken, which was another daily special and very good indeed.

The desserts are homemade, and I can attest that the chocolate mousse was very good. The other one that was ordered, a peanut butter cream pie, I can't speak for, as putting peanut butter and sugar together makes me shudder, but everyone else at the table thought it was great.

The evening was a surprise, and all the more fun for that. Trail's End would be a good place to go and hang out when you get the Hamptons horrors, which will happen soon enough now that spring and gridlock traffic are here.

May 2001

West Lake Clam and Chowder House

West Lake Marina

Montauk

668-6252

Breakfast, lunch, and dinner seven days in season; weekends year-round.

No reservations.

With the arrival of three or four excellent new restaurants this year, dining out east of the Shinnecock Canal continues to improve by leaps and bounds. But with Labor Day bringing the official end of summer I wanted to go somewhere to eat this week that represented what the South Fork is all about, at least for some of us.

I didn't want *amuses bouches* or wrist-straining wine lists, I didn't want three waiters hovering behind my chair or a plate decorated with Abstract Expressionist raspberry coulis. I wanted simple fresh food, a water view, and people having a good time, preferably somewhere I had never been before.

Which is how five of us found ourselves at the West Lake Clam and Chowder House in Montauk Sunday having a whale of a time and a meal whose sophistication really took us by surprise — Japanese, Chinese, Cajun, Thai, there was a bit of everything.

There was also a happy, good-natured crowd but a surprisingly short wait for a table (they don't take reservations).

The restaurant is a little waterside shingled hut in the middle of the Westlake Marina with an inside bar and dining area, an outside bar decorated with a frieze of dried starfish, a sushi bar, an outside dining area, and a number of tables beyond that, where you can sit with a drink and look at the water.

Which is what you will do all evening, because the view over Lake Montauk is splendid. On Sunday the lake, as calm as a mirror, reflected the sky as it changed from rose to strawberry sorbet. Hundreds of small boats faded from view in the dusk, to be replaced by points of light all around the lake.

What had given us a hint that the restaurant might be more than its name implied was the sushi. For price comparisons, the sushi platters are $11.50 (six assorted pieces and a California roll) or $14.50 (nine pieces and a California roll).

There is a raw bar and a range of sandwiches, salads, appetizers, and entrees that start at $2.50 for a cup of chowder (the New England is very good) and don't go much higher than $18 for the biggest portion of striped bass around. Wines by the glass are $5. But the place to look for the food is the daily specials board.

The high point of the evening — a deep-fried whole sea bass — cost $10. There was a more expensive version as an entree, but judging by the size of the appetizer, I would only order it if you are very hungry. The crisp, browned fish arrived stuffed with ginger, with a ginger and orange dipping sauce, its mouth full of parsley, and cherry tomatoes in place of eyes. It tasted even better than it looked.

We tried clams on the half shell and chowder and another terrific dish — spicy blackened cubes of swordfish with a dipping sauce. Also highly recommended are the little tender pork shumai dumplings and, if the yellowtail sushi and eel with avocado roll are anything to go by, any of the sushi.

The striped bass just missed perfection by being a fraction overcooked. It was served atop a portion of very good mashed potatoes which in turn were on top of a pile of perfectly cooked slivers of green and yellow squash. On the other hand, you would have to go a long way to find better grilled swordfish, which had just the slightest peppery kick to it.

One of our diners wanted soft shell crabs, but not as a sandwich, which was the way it appeared on the menu. The kitchen obligingly served the ultra crunchy critters on a nice bed of salad instead. The stuffed shrimp with pasta had a lot of flavor but lacked the just-out-of-the-water excitement of some of the other dishes.

The Chowder House makes its own desserts — Key lime pie, cheesecake, a fruit cobbler of some kind, and tiramisù — but we were too full to try any of them. About the only complaint I had of the evening was that they put whipped cream and a maraschino cherry on the top of a pina colada, sending what was already over the top completely over the edge.

Somehow the West Lake Clam and Chowder House has slipped under my radar until now, which makes me suspect that people who know about it have been trying to keep it to themselves. So I apologize to them for this review, which will let a few more people know about a very good thing.

August 2002

Sag Harbor &
Noyac

THE AMERICAN HOTEL

Main Street
Sag Harbor
725-3535
Lunch and dinner seven days. Reservations a day in advance.

There is a whole range of restaurants on the South Fork, from outdoor shacks to the overpriced and pretentious to the occasional first-rate gem. And then there is the American Hotel.

The sense of stepping back into the past as you go in through the front door is no illusion, no fake mock-up by Restaurants Incorporated, for the hotel is the oldest continuous business in Sag Harbor.

It is full of history. During the Revolution, when the wooden building that preceded the present one, known as James Howell's Inn, was being used by the British as their headquarters, Col. Jonathan Meigs surprised the British while they slept in their beds and captured them all.

From 1825 to 1845, the building was used by the cabinet maker Nathan Tinker until, along with the rest of Main Street, it burned down. The present building went up the following year as a two-family house, split down the middle for Tinker and his son, and in 1876 it was converted to a hotel, which it has remained ever since. Mark Twain and Henry Ward Beecher stayed there, as did Mary Pickford.

The hotel remained in the hands of the same family until it came to a standstill at the end of the 1960s, unused and undusted, with the last owner camping out in the dining room until his death at the age of 90. The present owner, Ted Conklin, bought the hotel and restored it to its polished mahogany glory in 1972.

There are a bar and lounge and three separate dining rooms decorated with comforting Victoriana, mementos of Sag Harbor's past, and the prettiest Art Deco lamps you could imagine. One of the dining rooms has a grand piano. Music in restaurants can be infuriating, especially if there is already too much noise, but the pianist at the American Hotel is aworth listening to.

The hotel's main claim to fame is its wine cellar, reputed to be the best not only on the East End but possibly on the whole of

Long Island. The wine list has a heft like the Shorter Oxford Dictionary and if you were to name a wine at random, you'd probably find it. But the list also includes plenty of inexpensive wines from every region, including a very nice Moulin-à-Vent Beaujolais at $28.

The menu may engender a moment of panic when you see the listings for caviar, but a closer look reveals the general prices to be less than fearsome. Appetizers are about $8 to $14, entrees nearly all in the mid-$20s, with just a couple of dishes over $30.

Most of the emphasis is on the main course, with a small but sensible choice of appetizers. It's not often that I would recommend choosing a salad over something more interesting, but the hotel's mache and endive salad with Gorgonzola and walnuts ($10) is so fresh and so beautifully prepared, with the mache cradled in a big radicchio leaf propped up by a little log stack of endive, that this is an exception.

In fact, all the appetizers were beautifully presented. Smoked salmon, of supreme quality, came with little servings of chopped hard-boiled egg, onion, sour cream, capers, cornichons, and two tiny blinis. The rich and subtle risotto was showered with fresh vegetables in a pretty bowl.

The homemade terrine is a very good value for $10, a hearty slab of pistachio-encrusted, high-calorie indulgence with a fruity sauce, pickles, and an elegant slice of crispbread. The diner who chose Little Neck clams for his appetizer, though unwilling to share them with the reviewer, reported them to be unusually sweet and good.

The American Hotel is one of the few East End places to serve sweetbreads — if you like them, then you like them very much. Who knows, with all these mad cow scares, they may disappear from menus altogether, so I'd grab them while the going is good if I were you.

The filet mignon was wonderful and, for $28, very big. Like most of the other dishes it came with meticulously prepared vegetables — green beans, snap peas, pureed squash, and potatoes being the ones I remember.

We ordered two fish dishes, salmon and the fish of the day, weakfish. The salmon was as good as it gets, and interestingly served in two pieces with a little pile of different roe on each. The weakfish was okay, but a little dull (that may be the reason it's called weakfish — it always seems to be a little dull).

The other special of the day we tried was a navarin of lamb, which came in a rich, fruity reduction sauce with an interesting edge to it. The melange of vegetables that came with it included baby onions and baby potatoes.

While all this was going on, glasses were discreetly filled and, for a second bottle of identical wine, a clean glass was brought so that it could be tasted. The service is very professional.

Of the two desserts we tried, the crepes with a lightly flavored crème Chantilly was a winner, once again as pretty as a picture. The other was a chocolate cake that was voted too sweet and too rich, which is not to say we'd have turned it down if our appetites had not already been satisfied.

Another chance to test the hotel's reputation for good service arose when, being practically innumerate, I made a mistake about the tip at the end of the meal. I've done it before and it's always interesting to see how a restaurant handles the embarrassing task of sounding out whether the discrepancy was a mistake or not. The hotel's maitre d' did it with total grace.

The American Hotel is no longer the inexpensive hangout for local writers it once was — the Petrossian caviar, cigars, Christofle silver, and Limoges china for sale in its shop give an idea of the clientele it now aims to reach — but it has gotten over the bumpy ride it had a couple of years ago, personified by a gold-chain wearing maitre d'hotel.

The food is excellent, and, compared to prices charged for far less by other places, it no longer seems particularly expensive. The service and ambience are always good, but at their best they make the customer feel cosseted and pampered like a favorite grandchild.

Wrapped in a cocoon of soft lighting, good wine, and delicious food, with a pianist quietly noodling away at Django Reinhardt's "Nuages," your crashed tech stocks and other cares of the world seem far away. It's a gracious way to spend an evening.

March 2001

THE BEACON

8 Water Street
Sag Harbor
725-7088
Dinner seven days except spring and fall. Seasonal.

Judging by the traffic backed up right over the bridge and onto North Haven Saturday night, Sag Harbor has to relinquish its title as the non-Hampton. Like it or not, it's the hottest spot on the South Fork.

But visitors tend to stick to Main Street, so there is still a chance of finding a table at the restaurant with the best view in the village. The Beacon is tucked away on Water Street and gives no sign from the road of what it is like once you have climbed the stairs to the second floor.

Then you see the North Haven Bridge and the whole of Sag Harbor Cove, with its marinas and greedy cormorants, and, beyond, Long Beach and the setting sun. There is an indoor bar, but bar patrons can sit and drink on the outdoor deck.

The news gets better when you find out that the food is as good as the view.

Now, it's not cheap — I have a particular quibble that the cheapest red wine listed cost $34 — but at the end of the meal none of us felt that we had not had good value for the money.

The Beacon does not take reservations, but as we were five people, an extremely obliging person on the other end of the phone put our name on a list and assured us that we were unlikely to have to wait very long. As it turned out we didn't have to wait at all. If you want to eat on the deck, which would obviously be the first choice if the weather is fine, then your party must be four or less.

As the $34 pinot noir we ordered had sold out, the management obligingly gave us a very nice Wölffer Estate Vineyards merlot, which was more expensive, for the same price.

The last time I ate at the Beacon, and possibly the reason I had not returned since, there had been extremely loud music. This time, bless them a thousand times over, there was no music at all. We could have a conversation.

Appetizers are $8 to $12; entrees are $16 (burger and fries) to $29 for filet mignon, though the menu is constantly changing according to what is in season. I must mention the particularly nice bread, a small thing, but important when you arrive ravenously hungry and know your fellow guests will take three months to decide what they want to order.

After a while the sun was decorated with some particularly photogenic pink clouds and we were launched into some very good appetizers. At last, a tuna tartare ($12) with some bite to it! A bite provided by sharp, fruity capers, big fat mustard seeds, and red curry paste.

We tried two excellent salads, one of smoked, shredded duck with greens, pumpkin seeds, dried cranberries, and a little goat cheese crostini on the side ($10). The other was a delicious mix of endive, radicchio, romaine, pears, and toasted pecans.

We did, in fact, try a third salad: wedges of iceberg lettuce, tomatoes, red onions, cucumbers, and a vinaigrette on the side with some rather dull Roquefort ($8). Chosen by a member of our dining team who doesn't like to share his food all around the table, he rightly guessed that no one would be hovering over his plate with a fork. It was what it was.

The beef carpaccio, on the other hand, was wonderfully delicate in flavor, served with a nice little salad of arugula and perked up with white truffle oil ($12).

As the fat, red disk of the sun dropped out of the clouds and slipped below the horizon and the lights of the harbor boats blinked on one by one, we were in a real Sag Harbor summer mood.

There was a really spiffy pasta dish of rigatoni, roasted tomato, bread crumbs, and goat cheese with long, thin, very spicy Merquez sausages ($19), and sweet pan-seared scallops served with an unusual mixture of avocado, cold fingerling potatoes, and tomato salad ($29).

The first mouthful of the halibut baked in parchment ($27) seemed a little bland, but once it was eaten in conjunction with the toasted couscous, sun-dried tomatoes, and tatsoi that accompanied it in its paper parcel, it was discovered to be just right, a perfect combination of flavors that resulted in an unusual and imaginative dish.

The filet mignon ($29) was perfect and the fries that accompanied it, in addition to a small arugula salad and Boursin cheese, were just amazing. Far too good to be called fries, they were definitely pommes frites. Top marks, too, for the sesame-crusted tuna, which was given a sharp contrast of a cabbage and jicama slaw.

We tried two desserts, a poached pear and a lemon pudding, which were fine but nothing special.

To sum up, the Beacon is the perfect summer dining spot, with a really pleasant and helpful waitstaff and very good food. It may be a couple of dollars more than some places, but it is worth it for the view alone.

July 2003

CHINDA'S

3284 Noyac Road

Noyac

725-1375

Dinner seven days.

I've always wondered why Chinda, whose restaurant has been around since the Boston Tea Party, chose to set up shop in the depths of Noyac.

The East End now has almost as many exotic restaurants as Ninth Avenue, but back then opening a year-round Thai restaurant on a dark road in Outer Sticksville would have seemed a foolhardy undertaking to most people. After all, this is a place where even restaurants in prime Main Street locations open and fold as quickly as a lousy poker hand.

But Chinda's has survived, and that means it's doing something right. And that something is undoubtedly its reasonable prices and good food.

It may be that the small dining room, with its very large menu, is propped up by the busy bar and takeout area at one side of the building, but I suspect that Chinda's has now established a faithful clientele for its stuffed chicken wings, tom yum koong soup, and other Thai favorites.

They don't come for the decor, which is fairly spartan, but being one of the few places on the East End that has Guinness on tap might be another draw.

On quiet evenings, check the specials board when you come in — you can be sure that these are the dishes that the chef, usually Chinda herself, has poised and ready to go.

Soups, like the lovely shrimp, mushroom, chili, lime, and lemon grass one mentioned above, are all $8.95 and are designed to be shared by two. Appetizers, which include spare ribs, squid salad, wontons, and curried fish cakes, run from $6.50 to $9.95, but most of them, too, are enough for two, or even three. Entrees are $13.95 to $15.95.

We didn't try those chicken wings this time, but can recommend them from other occasions. They are stuffed with bean

thread, bamboo shoots, dried mushrooms, and water chestnuts, and then deep-fried.

The chicken satay (you could also choose beef or pork), thin slices of marinated chicken on skewers served with peanut sauce, is always reliably good, as are the spring rolls. With their crisp, paper-thin coats, they are as far removed as can be imagined from the usual leaden doorstops masquerading under the name.

Also recommended is Mee Grob, a completely delicious pile of crisp noodles and fresh shrimp, topped with diaphanous bubbles of fried egg and served with a slightly sweet sauce.

Anyone unfamiliar with Thai food might want to choose Pad Thai as an introduction. It is not only Chinda's specialty entree but the Thai national dish, a warmly comforting combination of taste and texture in its mixture of rice noodles, shrimp, egg, bean curd, bean sprouts, and ground peanuts.

We tried Kai Pad Mamung Himapan, stir-fried chicken with cashew nuts, and Moo Pad Kana, a dish of pork in oyster sauce with very fresh broccoli, both of which were fine, if not quite as good as the Pad Thai. These three dishes were more than enough for five of us.

Remembered too from an earlier visit was a whole striped bass steamed with ginger and lemongrass and some interesting curries, but there are dozens of different pork, chicken, beef, and seafood dishes to choose from.

There is even some "English Food" — steak sausage pie, shepherd's pie, liver and bacon — though it sounded pretty unappetizing when compared to the delicate Thai cuisine.

We ended our meal with Chinda's signature sticky rice and mango, not to be missed, and a perfectly okay Key lime pie.

The food at Chinda's is exciting and fun and excellent value for the money. The restaurant is casual and comfortable, a friendly, unpretentious place where you can pick up the spring rolls with your fingers.

November 2002

DOCKSIDE BAR AND GRILL

26 Bay Street
Sag Harbor
725-7100
Lunch and dinner seven days. Breakfast Saturday and Sunday.

There have been some changes at the Dockside, but it is still the same friendly, funky place it has always been. Most people know it in summer, when its deck overlooking the harbor is one of the prettiest places to eat, but in the winter it takes on a different identity, a throwback to the time when Sag Harbor was a blue-collar town and not a fashionable escape for Manhattan's haute Bohemia.

It owes its funkiness to its status as both a restaurant and the Sag Harbor American Legion Hall. For one thing, it has the distinction of being the only restaurant on the South Fork whose lobby is flanked by official flag disposal boxes.

The layout of the tables in the main dining area is better now that there is a waist-high barrier separating it from the bar. The lighting is also greatly improved. The back dining room used to be carved out of the cavernous meeting hall by a barrier of trellis screens, which was a bit spooky. Now white paper is pinned floor to ceiling, making the space bright, enclosed, and very Christo-wraps-the-Reichstag.

There is a workmanlike wine list with a pretty good choice of reasonable wines by the glass, including a nice Chianti and the Bedell Cellars merlot that I often order and then remember too late I don't like.

The main change at the Dockside is that the menu is more adventurous than it used to be. There is an occasional entree special that is over $20, but on the whole all entrees are still under, starting with a $4.50 hamburger. Appetizers start at $5 for chili, chowder, or French onion soup; mussels, steamers, or shrimp quesadillas are $10.

On the night we were there, when the icy wind blowing off the water had one cursing one's lack of foresight in not being born in Tahiti, our good mood was restored when our waitress brought

us a complimentary plate of mussels baked with garlic, parsley, and breadcrumbs. They were wonderful. Do try them if they are on the menu (where they are somewhat confusingly labeled as "mussels scampi").

Then we further raised our spirits with garlic bread dripping with cheese and a couple of knockout appetizers. The spicy chicken wings ($8) were about as good as chicken wings can get. Paired with the full-flavored, crisp Caesar salad with plenty of shaved Pecorino Romano cheese ($7), they would have made a perfectly satisfactory meal.

An unusual appetizer special was the oyster pan roast — a very rich dish of oysters in cream that was a hit.

Although their rose red color was appropriately Christmassy, the rubbery pumpkin ravioli were less successful, mainly because their flavor was swamped by the fearsomely powerful sage leaves scattered over them.

Chicken pot pie has always been on the menu at the Dockside and it remains, probably wisely, the same bland, soothing dish that diners remember from childhood, before lemongrass and daikon radish were shipped around the country in plain brown wrappers.

The Dockside does a nicely presented paella piled into a flatbread wrapper, full of seafood and chorizo and well-cooked rice. Not quite the real thing but a passable imitation.

Both pastas we tried were excellent. One was on the regular menu, a simple pasta puttanesca made with fresh plum tomatoes lightly cooked with garlic, olives, and capers. The other was the Blue Plate Special, a marvelously flavorful concoction of linguine, clams, and mussels with a slightly smoky flavor and a hot final kick.

Another successful dish was the Hunter's Chicken, a simple dish of tender chicken in a rich wine sauce with tiny roast potatoes.

An acquaintance in the other dining room, whose table had taken every order of baby back ribs left in the kitchen, reported, by way of consolation, that they were excellent.

The Dockside is a favorite with many people, perhaps even more for the friendly ambience than the food; it's a perfect outdoor spot in summer, a small-town hangout in winter. But let's hope it has gone as far upmarket as it intends to go — we want good food, but let's keep the pinned-up paper, spelling mistakes on the menu, and the old guys at the bar.

January 2003

ESTIA'S LITTLE KITCHEN

1615 Bridgehampton–Sag Harbor Turnpike at Clay Pit Road

Sag Harbor

725-1045

Breakfast and lunch six days. Dinner Thursday through Sunday. Closed Tuesday.

Reservations for dinner only.

There are very few restaurants that don't have some kind of distinguishing feature that sets them apart from the rest of the pack, whether it be a wonderful wine list or a surly head waiter.

With Estia's Little Kitchen the emphasis is on the "little." This dollhouse-sized building on the Bridgehampton-Sag Harbor Turnpike is a popular breakfast and lunch place, but dinner turned out to be quite a revelation.

The restaurant is light-filled and informal and decorated with paintings and drawings of fish and surfcasting. One waitress can pretty much cope with the whole shebang.

The main room is divided into two small seating areas and a bar, but I had not noticed before that there is also a small room at the back, just large enough to hold a table for six.

It was like eating in a private house with your own personal chef. There was a companionable buzz from the next room, but we were free to talk to one another without shouting. It is not for those who go out to see and be seen, or for those who equate noise level with success, but we were knocked out by it, finding that it made the evening very special, particularly since the food turned out to be excellent as well.

Although they don't take reservations for breakfast or lunch, they do for dinner, so this might be a place to keep in mind for a special evening with friends. Those with pesky small children might keep it in mind also.

The menu includes two or three prix fixe entrees which include salad and dessert, such as linguine with broccoli rabe, braised beef with fettuccine, or salmon. The prices are between $19.95 and $21.95. On the evening we were there the prix fixe blackfish was sold out, so we were offered striped bass instead, a real bargain.

Appetizers are from $8 to $10 and include a couple of interesting salads and barbecued ribs. Entrees start with a $10 burger and fries at the low end and a $24 steak at the high end, with most being $20 or under.

Little Estia's crab cakes ($10 for two, which is another bargain) are terrific, with a charred crisp bread crumb crust and a subtle smoky seasoning that made them just a little different from the norm. They were served on top of a wonderful peppery cole slaw.

The turtle rolls ($8) were less successful. They are a combination of avocado, salsa, jack cheese, and other things wrapped in a tortilla and sliced. There were too many soft things and the flavors canceled each other out. The standard salad that came with the prix fixe dishes was just fine (the creative well has run dry when it comes to describing green salad).

All of our entrees were excellent with the one exception of the chicken bolognese with pappardelle. The pasta, made at the restaurant, was very good but the sauce was too bland. The other chicken dish, a breast flattened and somehow made hard and crunchy outside but tender and moist inside, could not have been plainer, but with good mashed potatoes, spinach, and a flavorful jus, it worked.

A word about that spinach. It seems like only yesterday that the universal treatment for spinach was to boil it to death, pulverize it, and then add a thick roux sauce. Now we have learned that all it needs is a bare minimum of cooking and a little gentle seasoning. Estia's does it to perfection.

The New York steak could not be faulted. It came with fries that were not crisp enough for the one who ordered them, but I have to admit that their tasty sogginess brought back English childhood memories and I really enjoyed them. All of them.

Another success story was the braised lamb shank ($19) with chard and butternut squash and a carrot and celery sauce. But the winning entree was definitely that striped bass, which was served with a kind of pumpkin tamale, a really original creation that set off the delicate flavor of the fish to perfection.

Desserts included a banana split, a huge plateful of sliced bananas, apple, pineapple, whipped cream, and three different

sorbets. And continuing the seasonal pumpkin theme, there was a fine pumpkin pie with a terrific pumpkin ice cream.

Estia's Little Kitchen, a bright and cheery place for a morning omelet, becomes intimate and relaxing at night. There is something very endearing about its smallness, and as the food is excellent, the wine choice good, and the service friendly and efficient, it is going on my list of places to eat when I am not on reviewing duty and can make my own choices.

November 2003

IL CAPUCCINO

Madison Street

Sag Harbor

725-2747

Dinner seven days. Reservations for five or more.

With everyone tearing their hair out about the disappearance of the South Fork's rural character, it's nice to find a few things that don't change: the Sag Harbor movie theater, say, or Bucket's Deli, or Il Capuccino, whose red-checked tablecloths and all-Italian menu have remained unaltered since the Jurassic.

Il Capuccino, housed in a couple of venerable Sag Harbor houses, is an interconnected series of dining rooms with pressed-tin ceilings, hanging Chianti bottles, wooden beams, candlelight, and the pungent aroma of its famous hot, oily garlic rolls.

It's not so much about comfort food, though the cuisine is basically that, as about mental comfort. Even if you are not Italian, it's like going home to Mother's, where no one expects you to be thin, clever, or well-dressed. And no one will object if you order a ceramic jug of the house wine instead of a bottle of Chateau Pretensioso.

Mind you, you are not going to throw up your hands in excitement when you see the menu, because even for an Italian restaurant it is remarkably conservative. Half of it is pasta; tomatoes and veal figure prominently. It is the sort of place where regulars settle on a dish they like and order it again and again.

The truth of this was borne out by a gentleman sitting near us on Saturday, who, when asked what he was eating, replied that it was chicken parmigiana, that he had been dining at the restaurant for 20 years, and that he never ordered anything else.

There is a choice of six salads between $3.95 and $6.95. The tomato and mozzarella salad is best ordered in summer, but even the vampire-ized tomatoes of winter are redeemed by one of the liveliest pestos around. The arugula, endive, radicchio, and goat cheese salad is a sure-fire winner, and the spinach with warm pancetta comes a close second.

A generous antipasto plate for $6.50 should really be shared between two. The $4.50 soup of the day was made with yellow and green squash, slightly creamy and with plenty of substance. Or you could start with mussels, clams in a white wine sauce, or fried calamari, any one of which is a reliable choice.

The entrees were rather less reliable. While the veal piccata ($17.95) was a hit, the blandness of the veal enlivened by a sharp lemon sauce, the dry and dull veal Milanese was coated with soggy, wet breadcrumbs and had to be returned.

We ordered two dishes with a tomato-based sauce, which meant that they were rather similar. One was shrimp (lots of shrimp) over angel hair pasta. The other was frutti di mare, a great heap of shrimp, mussels, clams, and squid over linguine. Both were good but did not meet with quite the enthusiasm of a friend eating nearby who ordered the daily special — penne with shrimp and sausage — and reported that it was light, well-balanced, and terrific.

Two regular specials were not on the menu on this occasion — osso buco and blackened catfish — but should they be, I can recommend them, particularly the osso buco.

For dessert, there's an excellent Italian cheesecake, quite different from the usual suspects, and a fine pistachio ice cream, but what was billed as a chocolate souffle with caramel sauce was a little gooey cake so sweet it almost gave me lockjaw.

Cozy. That's the word that sums up Il Capuccino. When there's a cold wind blowing across the bay and spring changes its mind about arriving, you don't want tile floors and hard-edged elegance, you want a hanging Chianti bottle and a basket of hot garlic rolls.

May 2002

JEFF AND EDDY'S

Main Street
Sag Harbor
725-0055
Breakfast, lunch, and dinner seven days. No reservations.

There's been quite a bit of curiosity about Jeff and Eddy's, situated as it is right in the middle of Sag Harbor's Main Street where every man and his dog could peer in through the windows as it was being renovated.

It was going be a fish restaurant, rumor said, but part of it was also going to be a fish market, one that stayed open late — that was a strike in its favor right away.

What could be seen through the windows didn't look particularly promising — dark wood, white tiled walls, naked heating pipes, pressed tin ceiling. What was this, nostalgia for the BMT? No, what the owners had in mind was an old New York City oyster bar, noisy and bustling and full of life.

And it works. The hub of the room is a big, horseshoe-shaped zinc bar, with the fish store visible behind it. On Friday, I had arrived early and, because they don't take reservations and they won't seat you until all your party is there, I sat at the bar and had a drink by myself. It is that rare animal, a place where you can be by yourself without feeling uncomfortable.

I fully intend to go there again at some quiet moment and sit at the bar with a Guinness, a dozen mixed oysters, and the Times Saturday puzzle. Though quiet moments, I suspect, may be rare.

Nearly all the tables are booths, providing privacy and a bit of a shield from the noise that mounts as the evening ages, the clientele gets younger and, we noted, looks better and wears less. Because with all that tile and tin it certainly is noisy.

But then it should be noisy, it's that kind of place. It is also the kind of capacious, funky bar that Sag Harbor needs and has lacked since the old Paradise went literary.

We found the service to be genuinely thoughtful, not the usual keep-the-punters-happy-and-move-them-along attitude.

By the time the rest of our party arrived there was only one table left, right by the kitchen. It was a 95-degree day and blasts of hot air came sweeping out of the kitchen like the sirocco (the chefs must have been as hot as their dishes).

When another table became free, we asked if we could move and our waitress, with no quibbling, moved us over. It made all the difference.

Prices? Our meal turned out to be surprisingly reasonable. A green salad is $4.50, fried clams, $9.75, fish and chips, $10.50, linguine with white clam sauce, $14.50, chicken, $14.50, lobster roll, $16, salmon, $17. A choice of two steaks at $28 and $32 were the most expensive items.

In keeping with the let's-all-make-a-lot-of-noise-and-party-all-night atmosphere, instead of quiet bread, they serve those sesame-seed-encrusted flatbreads so you can have internal as well as external noise.

Lunch is served from noon to 3 p.m. and offers a list of interesting sandwiches — fresh fish, oyster po' boy, whole belly clam — and burgers from about $7 to $12.

We began our meal with a good, crisp Caesar salad ($6.50) and a plate of mixed oysters and clams from the briskly cool fish store. The calamari in the grilled calamari salad ($7.50) had a wonderful flavor and were served on a nice little salad of watercress, green beans, olives, and slices of orange.

The South Fork fish chowder is well worth $5, full of fish and fine of flavor, though those people who do not like Manhattan clam chowder should be warned that its tomato-based stock makes it a close cousin.

We decided that our winning entree was the simple fish and chips, which was light and fresh and served with excellent fries and a fine, made-from-scratch coleslaw.

But close behind it, and a more interesting taste experience certainly, came the mixed grilled seafood skewers ($18), big chunks of swordfish, tuna, and salmon on a bed of scented jasmine rice.

The fish of the day was a huge slice of halibut that I know would have been wonderful but that had been allowed to cook just that little too long. Steamers ($11.50) were perfect, served in their natural broth with a little pot of herbed butter. But there could have been a couple more of them.

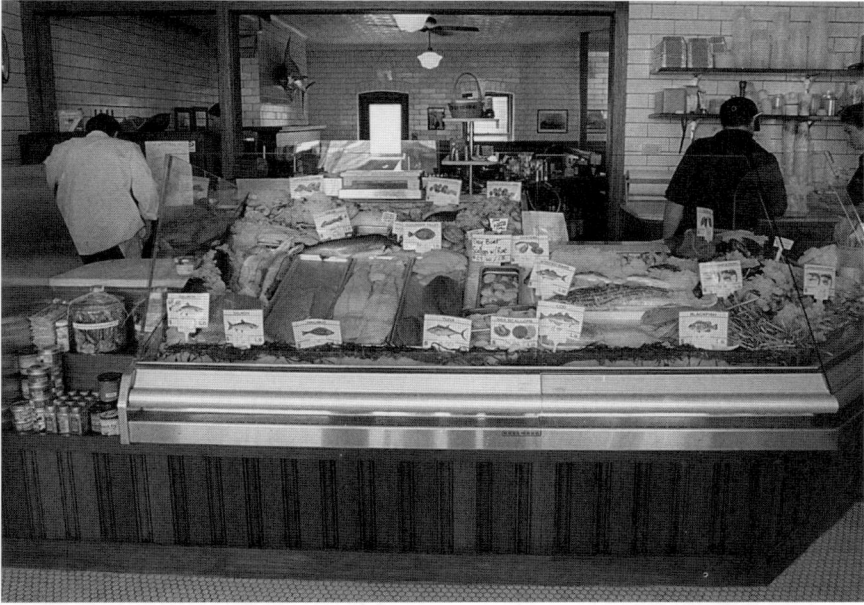

Desserts are made on the premises. They include a little round Boston cream pie, which was delicious though not very like Boston cream pie, and a Key lime pie, which was delicious but not very like Key lime pie. Maybe they should be called Sag Harbor cream pie and Sag Harbor lime pie.

It doesn't matter how good the food is, a restaurant has to have a certain unnameable quality, a combination of atmosphere, food, and service, before you put it on your short list of places to meet with friends.

Jeff and Eddy's has made it to mine, though it will probably be for midweek visits. Judging by the crowd on Friday, when the restaurant had only been open a week, I suspect weekends will be, well, good and noisy.

July 2003

OASIS

3253 Noyac Road

Noyac

725-7110

Dinner seven days. Brunch Sunday.

Running a restaurant on the East End is a far cry from running one on the Upper East Side of Manhattan. There's a short frantic season when you can't find waitstaff, followed by a long chill winter when a mournful wind blows around the empty tables. Allowances have to be made.

So if a new restaurant comes along where there is no call for allowances, where you can pull out all the stops and give it a wholehearted rave, then whoop-di-doo. It doesn't happen often, but Oasis on Noyac Road fits the bill.

Oasis has taken over the odd building overlooking Noyac Bay that was Jessup's by the Bay and, before that, the Inn at Mill Creek. The view is charming, the decor simple, and the acoustics are good. The service is efficient and unobtrusive.

There is an interesting and carefully chosen wine list with plenty of reasonable choices, a large selection of wines by the glass, and very good value over all. The list also offers a smile or two; one of the wines listed is called "Fat Bastard" and another is "Old Fart," with a picture of an irascible elderly gent on the label.

But it is the food that steals the show. The menu, which has about eight starters and eight entrees with a few daily specials, is imaginative without being over the top and steers away from the trendy dishes that have become clichés — no seared tuna, no calamari.

Appetizers start at $7 for a yellow tomato gazpacho with grilled shrimp and avocado and rise to $12 for smoked lobster with truffle, leek, and potato salad with tarragon cream. Entrees are from $22 for chicken to $30 for a grilled Black Angus steak. Local oysters and Little Neck clams on the half shell follow market price. The portions are just the right size, neither appetite-destroyingly large nor disappointingly small.

When the appetizers arrived at the table, their beautiful presentation brought a sudden expectant hush. Was this going to be a winner? The meal you hope you're going to get but very seldom do?

A special of the day was an intensely flavored cold asparagus soup with crabmeat and perfectly cooked asparagus tips. From the vivid beechleaf green of its color to the creamy delicacy of its taste, it was the perfect summer soup (though I admit that the yellow gazpacho sounds wonderful, too).

Then there was a perfect little tomato and goat cheese tart, topped with basil and frisée, that was a masterful combination of different textures, and sweet contrasted with sharp. And a peppy shrimp ceviche with marinated onions and chili peppers. By then our reviewing team was making excited noises.

Finally, there was the smoked lobster, which was still lobster, but lobster exaggerated, lobster with 1,600 on its SATs. The excited noises turned to coos.

The presentation of the entrees was equally appealing, the consumption of the entrees was equally rewarding.

Grilled scallops — grilled with force and full of flavor — were served over an island of perfectly cooked corn and parsley risotto in a pond of vivid carrot sauce. The plainest and least expensive dish, a roast chicken breast with shallot mashed potato, spinach, and a thyme-flavored juice, was simplicity itself and faultless.

The one dish that got less than a rave was the bouillabaisse. It was very good, the saffron broth was nice, the croutons with rouille were fine, but it was just not very exciting. At least not compared to the striped bass braised with purple potato, chorizo, cockles, and green olives, which set the pulse racing with its knockout combination of flavors, including a chorizo of exceptionally good quality.

But the winner of the evening was the swordfish. This you have to try. Instead of being served in a thin, rapidly cooked slice, as it usually is, Chef John P. Donnelly cooks it in a two-inch-high chunk, crusted in Parmesan, and served over escarole and white beans with a yellow tomato sauce.

It must have taken a fair bit of experimentation to get this right, but it becomes another animal altogether, a real eye-opener.

And Oasis doesn't drop the ball when it comes to dessert. The dishes are simple — banana bread pudding, apple fritters, rhubarb crumble — but they are elevated to a higher plane. I particularly recommend the crème brûlée taster, with its three little pots of vanilla, coffee, and chocolate, each one with a delicate sugary crust served at the right temperature.

The rhubarb crumble contrasts a sharp, tart filling with a sweet crumble and ice cream, and a small chocolate and peanut butter cake was, I was assured (I don't eat peanuts and sugar together), just as good as they had hoped.

We hung around for a long time over coffee, which is what you do when you have enjoyed your meal from start to finish, rather than grabbing the check and heading for the door, which is what you do when you haven't.

Oasis. I know it's on the tedious Noyac Road, but put it on your list. It's an Oscar.

July 2002

THE PARADISE CAFE

126 Main Street
Sag Harbor
725-6080
Dinner seven days. Brunch Friday, Saturday, and Sunday.

When a restaurant gets a good reputation it brings with it the burden of customers' high expectations. Pleasant surprise is no longer a factor, but dashed expectations are.

So it was with a slight twinge of apprehension that I headed out into the snow to eat at the New Paradise Cafe in Sag Harbor, which has been taken over by Robert Durkin of Robert's in Water Mill, one of the South Fork's best restaurants. What our crew was hoping for was similarly good, imaginative food but in a more informal setting and with slightly lower prices.

Great was the relief, then, as the meal ended upon a gingerbread bread pudding of such splendor it could take its place in this holiday season alongside frankincense and myrrh, and we all agreed that Mr. Durkin had come through in spades.

Thanks to the rather utopian vision of the previous owner, he has the challenge of one of the most unwieldy restaurant spaces around. The front, and best-shaped third, is a bookstore. I imagine the symbiosis — "Mabel, I'll just pick up a paperback while we wait for our table" and "Mabel, I've got my Michael Crichton, what about a chocolate martini while we're here?" — is in the bookstore's favor. (The bookstore expands onto the second floor.)

Then comes a wee space with one table and the reservation desk, whose occupant is in danger of being crushed by the cheery crowd at the long, copper-covered bar. Once you have navigated the bar you arrive at the narrow dining room, which has been lightened by painting the mahogany wainscoting.

To illustrate the difficulties of the space, if you stand at the end of the room, next to the door to the popular summer patio, you can see that there is a four-inch slope to the floor. But it has some interesting lighting, a feel of the 1920s, and will soon have cushioned oak chairs.

I like the way the wine list is arranged: wines by the glass ($7 to $9.50), local, West Coast, and international for both reds and whites. By the bottle, there are a lot of whites under $30; the reds are more serious, with enough inexpensive ones for slimmer wallets, but rather more special-occasion wines. Which is the way it should be.

The waitstaff were professional way beyond cafe standards — no thumbs in the soup here. Not only were they efficient, but discreet to the point where I noticed that our waitress, arriving to tell us the specials in the middle of an anecdote, tactfully retreated until after the punch line.

Although the menu changes often, appetizers are about $7 to $11 and entrees $12.50 (burger, fully loaded) to $27 for steak. Not the cheapest menu on the block but considerably below many places of similar quality.

The special appetizer of the day was fresh sardines, escabeche-style, cooked and then served cold after being in a light marinade overnight — I suspect white wine, herbs, garlic, and vinegar, though I didn't check. As were all the appetizers, it was terrific.

Two items on the menu which are highly recommended are the hot-pepper shrimp served in the shell, very spicy, and with plenty of peppery sauce to mop up with bread, and, even better, the garlic snails on soft polenta. The contrast between the strongly flavored snails and the creamy, slightly lumpy polenta was a real kick. The polenta was amazingly good.

Paradise also does a mean couscous and, although we didn't try it, this bodes well for the risotto, which is different every day.

For those who prefer to start with a salad, the two we tried — one of arugula with roasted pears, Roquefort, and walnuts and another of escarole, sweet peppers, goat cheese, and black olives in a blood orange vinaigrette — were equally good.

The entrees were not as exciting as the appetizers and the desserts, but there were certainly no complaints. Our top vote went to a beautifully cooked duck with raspberries and wild rice.

Every evening there is a whole grilled fish served with Chinese black bean sauce, and on Saturday it was red snapper of a size definitely more for two people than one. The grilled tuna arrived a little more cooked than had been requested, but nonetheless was very moist. In addition to that admirable couscous, it came with some wonderful oven-dried tomatoes that made an appearance with a number of dishes.

For a one-dish meal, you could hardly do better than the fresh lobster Cobb salad, a hearty mix of frisée, lobster, avocado, roasted bacon (crisp, thick cut, not greasy), and those tomatoes again. With its fresh mayonnaise-based Louis dressing it felt very California and sunny. For pasta lovers, the penne with veal was subtle and not at all heavy.

If there is anything calculated to give a reviewer writer's block it is the average South Fork dessert menu and the impossibility of finding a new adjective for flourless chocolate cake. But the desserts we tried — that gingerbread pudding and a little banana brûlée tart — had the superlatives flowing in a way that would have warmed Mr. Roget's heart.

The Paradise will continue to open for lunch and weekend brunch. The lunch menu has a big selection of salads and hot and cold sandwiches, mussels, fish and chips, salmon cakes, hot-pepper shrimp, and such, and prices go from $6 to $14.50. Brunch offers eggs pretty much any way you can imagine, waffles, pancakes, and French toast, plus most of the lunch menu.

There is also a bar menu — useful to know about if you are on your way to the movies — of about a dozen items, ranging from a spicy calamari salad to a burger, with prices from $7.50 to $13.

Awkward space or not, I think this incarnation of the Paradise can hardly fail to be a success. I imagine that on its wish list would be that the bookstore eventually move to a more appropriate spot so the cafe can reclaim its lost territory. Then we'll really be talking.

December 2002

SHELTER ISLAND

OLDE COUNTRY INN

11 Stearns Point Road
Shelter Island
749-1633
Dinner seven days. Lunch Saturday and Sunday.

Well, here's one that completely slipped in under the radar — one of the most pleasant places to have dinner outdoors around here, and no one we asked had even heard of it! (Except, of course, all those we saw eating there on Saturday, and they'd probably prefer it stayed that way.)

The late 1800s Olde Country Inn, on a quiet road just a short walk from Crescent Beach, is newly restored. The rambling building has deep wraparound porches with wicker furniture, a tower, and all the frilly bits of its period. The atmosphere is New England rather than the Hamptons.

The outdoor dining area, which overlooks the back gardens, is arranged on different levels, with some tables along the porch, some under umbrellas on a lower deck, and most under a charming pavilion decorated with little lights.

The pretty table settings indicate a certain formality, but we noticed that all the guests were casually dressed and the speedy and efficient waitstaff couldn't have been more friendly and accommodating.

It became apparent that this wasn't a chips-and-a-beer place once we saw the menu and the very respectable wine list: reasonable prices, though you can have a Chateau Margaux if you want, and a special section of Long Island wines. A lovely Cotes du Rhone — Domaine de la Solitude, who could resist the name? — was $24.

Menu prices are about par for the Hamptons course, $6 to $11.50 for appetizers and $16.75 (penne with vegetables) to $29.50 (Dover sole) for entrees.

Your basic mesclun salad is very nicely done here with a carefully balanced dressing, and the soup of the day, a cold leek and potato soup, was perked up by the addition of celery to give it a bit of a kick. A warm salad of red and yellow beets, leeks, and sliced fresh artichokes is also a pleasant way to start the meal.

The Maryland crab cake ($11.50) was more a compilation of crab than an actual cake, but it was very good. The tuna tartare, on the other hand, was a little strange as the fish was mixed with a rather strong mayonnaise.

Undeterred by the hot weather, we laid waste a number of hearty entrees more suitable to a meal around the fireplace than outside among the fireflies, including a magnificent osso buco and a generous portion of rack of lamb with gratin dauphinoise.

But the dish of the evening was unanimously voted the calf's liver and mashed potatoes. I know that not everyone likes it, but the Olde Country Inn's liver could convert even the most skeptical.

The fish of the day — swordfish, served in well-seasoned and moist cubes over a rather mundane couscous — was good, but the dull-sounding boneless chicken breast was flawless, served with perfectly cooked polenta, broccolini, and "wild" mushrooms that had so much taste one could almost believe it.

As the moon crept across the unseasonably hazy sky we hung around drinking coffee and picking at a wonderful strawberry Melba (no doubt about these strawberries being local) until nearly everyone else had left.

It had been outdoor dining the way it should be.

Would you make the trip there from Montauk? Maybe not. But if you are one of those who likes to take the ferry and get away from the summer chaos, then you should add it to your list.

July 2001

THE RAM'S HEAD INN

Ram Island
Shelter Island
749-0811
Dinner seven days. Brunch Sunday. Seasonal.

There are few more romantic places on the East End to watch the sun go down than the Ram's Head Inn on Shelter Island. But if you go for brunch, you can expand the meal into a mini-vacation.

Our trip on Sunday included a voyage on the spiffy new Southern Star ferry, a stop to watch two ospreys mating on the Ram Island causeway, and a tour to choose the cutest waterside cottage and the ugliest post-modern excess.

Certainly when you have crossed the causeway onto the little hiccup of land that is Ram Island, you feel a million miles from the biggest-is-best Hamptons.

The inn, with its old-fashioned chintz-decorated formality, was the setting for "Bringing up Baby," that classic screwball comedy starring Katharine Hepburn and Cary Grant. Or maybe it was "White Christmas." (And please don't write to disillusion me.)

By coincidence, it turned out that two members of our party had been married at the Ram's Head seven years earlier, and so the romantic aspects of the inn got rather more play than they would have otherwise. Since they are still billing and cooing like newlyweds, it seems a good advertisement.

The inn has lawns and gardens spreading down the hill toward the water, and trees with swings, and a long verandah where you can sit outside and enjoy a drink, so obviously a warm summer day is the best time to visit. But it was almost as enjoyable in April, when there were blazing fires to keep away the chill and daffodils wherever you looked.

Brunch is really more like lunch, with the dining room filling up rather late, and prices are similar to the dinner menu: $7 to $14 for appetizers and $14 to $21 for entrees.

A free mimosa or bloody mary is offered with all breakfast items and a basket of tiny hot raisin muffins starts the meal.

Highly recommended, either as an appetizer or a main course, is the $14 crab cake. It was terrific, and beautifully served with a

sprinkling of zippy little black beans, Vidalia onion relish, and a pickled lime and avocado remoulade.

The spring pea and butter lettuce soup was soothing and rustic, and there were two superlative salads. One was an excellent mixed green salad with pencil-shavings of beet-root. The other, with Romaine lettuce, capers, and lemon garlic vinaigrette, came with an impressive confit of whole tomatoes and the most divine, crunchy Parmesan tuiles (like a crisp, paper-thin cookie). They were so good we had too order one for each of us.

Of the entrees, perhaps the simplest — scrambled eggs with brie and chives — was the best. An omelet with shavings of prosciutto was also excellent, as was a very light pasta with asparagus, mushrooms, and kalamata olives in a fresh tomato sauce.

One of the specials of the day was salmon, which was rather overcooked, and the poached eggs with lobster and pea hash was a little bland and somehow just didn't get its act together. Nothing the matter with the home fries, though.

We wouldn't have tried a dessert at all — after all, it was lunch time — if one member of our party hadn't turned ugly about it and we were forced to give in to her to avoid a scene.

Let me tell you about that dessert: There was a layer of almond and meringue dacquoise — slightly chewy, slightly crunchy — sandwiched between a rich chocolate and almond truffle cake of immaculate flavor and texture. A sharp apricot sauce and a sprinkling of blackberries and blueberries provided a vivid contrast. I vote it the best dessert I've had all year.

Ideally, the 11-mile loop at the Nature Conservancy's Mashomack Preserve should have been included in the day's outing, so we could have walked off the dessert. But there were no volunteers.

What you get at the Ram's Head Inn is more than just the food — which is excellent but not earth-shattering — it's the trip, the island, the ambience, and the view as well.

Come August, when you've just spent 30 minutes looking for a parking space in Sag Harbor, a trip to the inn might just save your sanity.

April 2000

SUNSET BEACH

Shore Road
Shelter Island
749-3000
Until July 1, open for dinner Friday through Monday.
Dinner seven days fter July 1.

You don't really want to go all the way to Shelter Island for dinner, do you?

You'll have to go across the North Haven bridge and the ferry, however charming, adds to the dinner bill, and you can easily get lost on the way to Crescent Beach, even though it is worth the trip.

I thought not. So just ignore what follows about the Sunset Beach restaurant, because this is one place I wouldn't mind keeping to myself.

There's nothing like a trip on the ferry and across the island to unwind from Hamptons hassle. I had been given a choice of a table at 6:30 or 8:30 on Saturday, and had opted for the earlier time, when there were still a few swimmers breaking the smooth waters of the bay.

The restaurant is built on three stepped rooftops, separated from the beach only by a narrow road, and it looks as if it has been scooped up by a tornado from the South of France or the West Indies to find itself, rather surprised, on staid Shelter Island.

Under new ownership, it now has tables on the ground floor and chairs scattered around on the sand for drinks, but the main action is upstairs. The first rooftop step is an agreeable louche bar, the next step is a dining room which is open on all sides with a covered roof, and the last step, up among the treetops, is an open deck topped only by strings of lanterns.

The atmosphere is casual, the tables are covered with oilcloths printed with lurid tropical fruit, and the attractive young waitstaff wear everything from '50s retro to what looked like a small face-cloth held on by a couple of shoelaces. Charm, pizzazz, laid-back cool — Sunset Beach has it in spades.

It became obvious that the 6:30/8:30 choice means that there are two sittings, one for the sunset watchers and the later time for the see-and-be-seen crowd, but by 9 we hadn't been given so much as a hint that we should move along.

Delighted to find ourselves seated on the top deck, we took our hastily hand-scrawled menus, ordered margaritas because it matched the mood, and settled back to enjoy the scenery, expecting a long wait and food that probably wouldn't match the view.

The menu turned out to be quite expensive. Appetizers start at $8 for a green salad and rise to $14 for tuna tataki, entrees range from an $18 angel hair pasta Provencal to $29 for steak frites.

One of our reviewing team, who hadn't eaten all day and was ravenous, laid into the bread and butter.

"Hey, this is wonderful bread. And the butter is amazing!"

And so it was — and there's no better clue to what is to follow than the bread and butter a restaurant chooses to serve.

So it wasn't really a surprise when the service turned out to be both fast and charming, though we were still a bit stunned by the quality of the food.

There was a wonderful roughly chopped gazpacho and a dish of chilled asparagus and tiny marinated tomatoes that was simple but perfect (though not cheap at $11).

Our favorite appetizer was the calamari salad, with its featherlight batter, cucumber sauce, and spaghetti-like frizz of carrot. Also some delicious Pacific rim shrimp rolls with a lively peanut dipping sauce. The tuna tataki, seared, rare, and served with a seaweed salad and ponzu sauce, was also very good.

Right in front of our table an osprey dived and came up with a fish in its claws. A few minutes later it returned and repeated the performance — it's presumably on a retainer.

Meanwhile a sudden scudding breeze swept across the bay, breaking up the summer calm into little teal blue ripples and ushering in an impressive black cloud stage left. The light changed, the colors changed, and in the distance the pink sky darkened and a rumble of thunder was heard. But by this time our faces were buried in our entrees and not even a snowstorm would have shifted us.

As with the appetizers, there wasn't a dud among them. Also, our hungry guest had ordered three side dishes, so by the end of the meal we had sampled practically everything on the menu.

Once again, attention to detail can tell you so much about a restaurant, and those side dishes were perfection: buttery roasted sweet corn stripped from the cob, lemon ginger spinach, and the most perfect jade green asparagus.

The moules frites ($22) are really great here; lots of places have good mussels but Sunset Beach's fries are arguably the best on the East End. A marinated ahi tuna ($26), served with asparagus and the most delicious jasmine rice, came in neck and neck with the wild striped bass ($24) — its skin seared golden, its delicate ichor trapped inside — which had an interesting lemon chili sauce.

Equally good were the fat browned sea scallops on their bed of corn and fava beans, though the winner, by a nose, was the superlative soft-shelled crab, which was so light, so crisp, so... ("Anyone in the newsroom fancy a lunch run to Shelter Island?")

The black cloud, having given us just a frisson of concern, passed to our right and, exactly on time, a mauve sun broke through the clouds, picked up some strength, turned the whole sky the color of strawberry jam, and went down in a blaze of hot red glory. The intense pressure of the colors on the retina were as pleasurable as the intense flavors on the palate.

A couple of desserts with enough spoons for everyone is usual reviewing protocol, but this wouldn't do for Miss Extremely Hungry, who insisted on a strawberry shortcake all to herself, so in the end — a blessed decision — we ordered four desserts.

Maybe that rumble of thunder, that sudden darkness and rushing wind, marked the passage through the sky of the great pastry god Caloricus, because the desserts at Sunset Beach are out of this world.

There was a hot chocolate gateau that had the lightness of a souffle, a sticky, caramelized pineapple tarte Tatin, a crème brûlée of silky perfection and delicate crust, and a shortcake that was buttery soft inside but had a biscuity crunch outside.

Just as we had finished moaning and groaning with pleasure over the last crumbs, a warm rain started and our waitress obligingly found us a table under cover where we could have coffee.

There are restaurants with good food and restaurants with good views and outdoor dining; you can find funky charm and good service, pleasant music and attractive bars, but you seldom find them all in one package. We discovered that the pastry chef, Lisa Murphy, and the chef, Terry Harwood, both of whom came recently from Los Angeles to run Sunset Beach, got married about a month ago. Maybe love has something to do with it.

Sunset Beach won't appeal to those who like their waiters and tablecloths starched, but for the rest of us, believe me, dining on the East End doesn't get much better than this.

June 2002

SWEET TOMATO'S
15 Grand Avenue
Shelter Island Heights
749-4114
Dinner six days. Closed Monday.

The center of Shelter Island may officially be that boring bit around Town Hall, but the soul of the place is surely Shelter Island Heights, which is a strong contender for the most interesting half-square-mile on the East End.

You reach it via a short causeway, with Chase Creek on one side and Dering Harbor on the other, and leave it, as often as not, on the North Ferry. The land rises steeply, each winding street lined with gingerbread-laden Victoriana, including the house with the famous leaning tower, and at the very top an unpaved road switchbacks through the woods beside a vertiginous drop with stunning views of the North Fork.

In the center of this friendly hodgepodge of an earlier century is a new restaurant called Sweet Tomato's, postcard pretty and slap in the middle of the action. Well, perhaps "action" is a little strong, but as close to action as the island gets.

There is a rich choice of restaurants on Shelter Island, but the fairly conservative Italian menu at Sweet Tomato's — pastas, chicken in sauce, veal in sauce — is guaranteed to have something for everyone. You can order a steak if you feel like it, between $21.95 and $23.95, but though the menu is heavy on seafood it is surprisingly weak on fish, flounder being the only representative (and flounder hardly counts).

I would say the prices are reasonable, all entrees but the steaks being under $20, but there are a few lapses — a couple of $9.95 salads, no appetizers under $8.95, and the two side orders of vegetables (entrees come without) are $6.95 and $7.95. The side orders are quite enough for two, however, and the broccoli rabe received rave reviews.

Although Sweet Tomato's has only been open a few weeks, it was packed on Saturday night and, unusually, it was still busy by the time we left — not an early bird special place, obviously. And we hear that the busy bar stays open until the small hours.

It is as pretty inside as it is out, light and airy and arranged on different levels. The service is fast and professional — no high schoolers wandering over with the wrong dish and looking blank when you ask for water.

Wines by the glass are reasonable, but the wine list seemed ill-advised. It is small, knowledgeably chosen, and each wine is offered at a fair price, but there are very few inexpensive ones and far too many high-priced ones for a restaurant of relative simplicity.

We started our meal with a marvelous bruschetta, fresh, piquant, and packing a hearty garlic punch. The fried calamari were also very good. Instead of the usual rather fierce, concentrated sauce they came with a light, hot marinara sauce that complemented the squid instead of overwhelming it.

The pear salad needs a little work. It came with big, unappetizing, quartered tomatoes and large chunks of Gorgonzola that dominated all the flavors.

Pasta is obviously Sweet Tomato's strong suit; 15 different ones are listed. The shrimp Domenico, which was shrimp, mushrooms, artichokes, and asparagus with penne, was terrific and we heard equal praise for a creamy fettuccine dish with shrimp, scallops, and spinach, which someone had tried a few nights before.

For something completely simple, the chicken francese, with its light, lemony sauce, could hardly have been improved upon. The classic veal marsala, on the other hand, was dull.

We also tried the lonely flounder, which was a very generous portion, perfectly nice, but with rather too much oregano for my taste.

A nice touch is that your waiter brings a tray of desserts to the table for you to choose from. We tried a pleasant chocolate and hazelnut torte and — really recommended — a lovely tiramisu.

The food is very good, though maybe they shouldn't hold their breath waiting for the guy from the Guide Michelin. What will bring diners back again and again, I suspect, is that everything at Sweet Tomato's is so welcoming, from its charming exterior to its friendly staff.

May 2003

Southampton &

North Sea

BASILICO

10 Windmill Lane
Southampton
283-7987
Lunch and dinner seven days. Sunday jazz brunch.

Basilico, on the corner of Job's Lane opposite Agawam Park, has been around for a dozen years now and is obviously here to stay.

The decor is quintessential Hamptons: tiled floors, light wood, white walls, undraped windows. In the daytime the space is bright and sunny and at night the effect is airy, but, thanks to extremely well-planned lighting, not chilly. Which is essential for winter dining because, let's face it, Southampton Village at night is hardly Rio de Janeiro when it comes to joie de vivre and revelers in the streets.

Visual highlights of the restaurant are attractive bottle racks behind the bar and a geometric display of handcrafted white ceramic plates with basil-leaf decorations in the dining room.

The downside of the hard-edged surfaces is that when the restaurant is full, it is noisy. The service was a little spotty on a recent quiet Sunday, it being one of those arrangements where there is one waitress who is run off her feet and one greeter who sits at the bar doing nothing.

The menu is of a sensible size and changes according to the season, with an emphasis on upscale pastas and pizzas and plenty of salads and daily specials.

Prices are up there. Apart from a $7 soup, appetizers range from $10.50 for grilled vegetables to $14 for herb-crusted goat cheese with roasted beets and haricot verts. Salads start at $8.50 for a green one and go up to $12.50 for spinach and endive with pecans and Gorgonzola; pastas are $17 to $25, and main dishes range from $24 for onion-crusted chicken to $28 for veal piccata or shell steak with garlic mashed potatoes.

The wine list, while full of good stuff, has few inexpensive choices. One of them was a fine $32 shiraz. Wines by the glass are $7.50 to $12.

Mushroom risotto might not leap to mind as an appetizer choice (and indeed the portion was generous enough to serve as

an entree) but this beautifully prepared and subtle dish was a treat — and a surprise. A well-prepared risotto is a rare bird on the East End.

Subtlety was also the word that came to mind for the soup of the day, which we were told was potato and leek but whose warm autumnal yellow color and ripe, peaty flavor alerted us to sweet potatoes rather than your run-of-the-mill Idahos.

But neither dish quite lived up to a ring of sliced portobello mushrooms, baked with a creamy Gorgonzola topping, which surrounded a small salad of radicchio and endive. It was simple and perfect.

Basilico has six different pizzas. There is a simple tomato and basil pie at $17 and a vegetable pizza at $18, but most are $20, including the house special: broccoli rabe, black olives, garlic, Gorgonzola, goat cheese, and mozzarella.

But if you were thinking of dropping in with the kids to share a pizza, you might first ponder the small print at the bottom of the menu, which reads, in part: "A $23 corkage fee will be charged for each bottle of wine brought onto the premises. An appropriate share plate charge will be added to all shared items. This restaurant is rated PG! Parental Guidance is a must!"

With regret we skipped the pizza to concentrate on fish, meat, and pasta.

The linguine with Little Neck clams ($25) was excellent. No clams from a can here. North America is particularly blessed with shellfish — 500 species on the Pacific Coast alone — but surely few can beat our Long Island clams. And if you can't eat them raw on the half shell with a squeeze of lemon, then cooking them up with white wine is a pretty good second choice.

The veal piccata with asparagus and roast potatoes ($28) was pleasant but a little pedestrian, and the special of the day, striped bass, was smothered in an overpowering olive and tomato sauce and served over a huge heap of barely seasoned lentils and greens. But the fish itself was terrific once it had been liberated.

As we finished our meal with a very nice fruit crisp and coffee, our feelings were that we had eaten well, but not exceptionally, and that the menu, as generically Hamptons as the decor, would have to demonstrate rather more originality to draw us back again for those prices.

November 2001

BELLES EAST

Elm Street

Southampton

204-0300

Dinner six nights. Closed Tuesday. Brunch and late night barbecue on weekends.

It's hard to analyze the exact ingredients that make a restaurant a hit, though heaven knows prospective restaurateurs twist themselves into knots trying.

On Friday, when we went to Southampton to Belles East, which is where the grungy and much-beloved Hansom House used to be, it was only the third weekend it had been open. Was it too soon for a review? Would anyone be there at all?

When we arrived, we were not sure if it was the right place, what with the elegant house, the bluestone entry, the landscaping, the valet parking, and the stream of young people coming and going. Since Belles has not had much publicity, it must have been word of mouth that had drawn them there.

First of all, Belles East bears virtually no relationship to the original Belles, a little shack serving Jamaican food perched on the edge of the tarmac at Gabreski Airport in Westhampton, except charm and good food.

The food at Belles East is mainly Creole, and the big restaurant has a warm New Orleans feel. The large bar is furnished with fat whorehouse sofas and the dining room, while it has clean, modern lines, has the dark wood and cream and burgundy color scheme of an old speakeasy.

At present Belles is just serving dinner on weekends, but soon the outdoor terraces will be open, hours will be extended, and brunch, lunch, and a late-night barbecue will be added. Live music starts about 9:30 p.m.

The wine list has about a dozen reds and a dozen whites, ranging from $20 to $76, and wines by the glass are $6 to $9. The cheapest reds are a delightful Cotes du Rhone called Les Bec Fins or an Australian shiraz called Woop Woop, both $26.

Because all the dishes we liked best were Creole and the ones we were less enthusiastic about were the run-of-the-mill staples

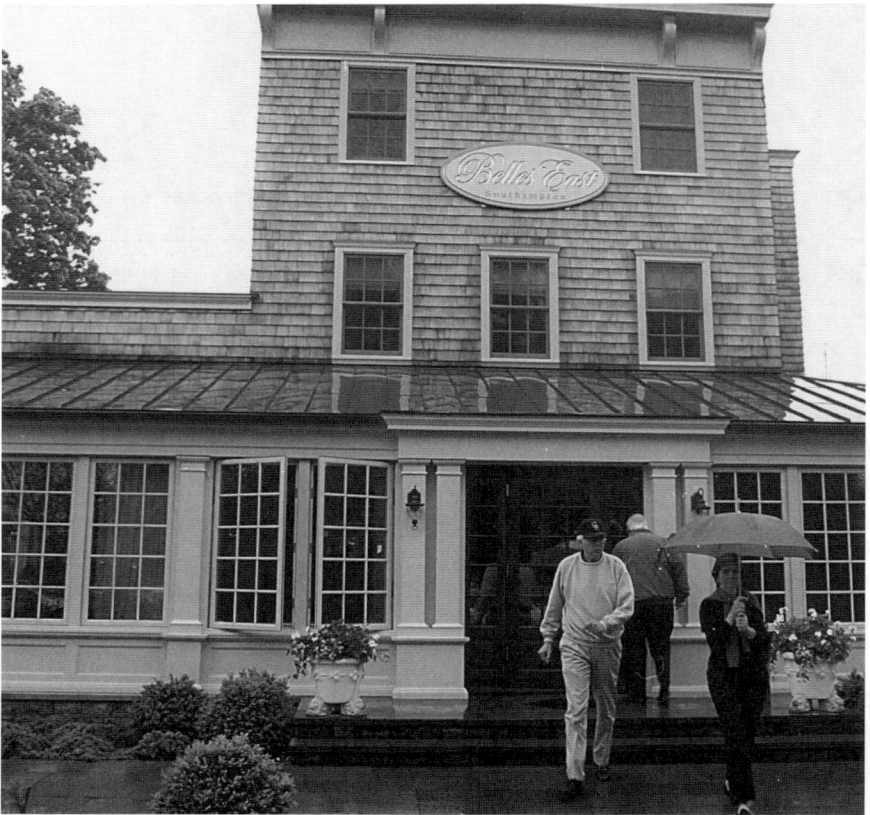

like tuna steak or steamed mussels, I would say stick with the Creole.

Appetizers run from $6 to $12, entrees from $18 to $26 (with the exception of a $38 20-ounce prime aged steak), and there is a raw bar.

The mussels, as I said, were, nyeh, okay, unless everyone else is eating a steaming gumbo ($10) redolent with that mysterious, musky filé powder made from dried sassafras leaves, or the wonderful hot, hot crawfish cakes ($9) with black-eyed pea salsa. In which case you sit and sulk and mutter under your breath, "I knew I should have chosen that."

One of the appetizers of the day was seared tuna carpaccio rolled in pepper, very light and pleasant. We also tried an outstanding salad of baby spinach, slices of mango, roasted pecans, and little rounds of baked goat cheese. It was $12, but worth every penny.

For our entrees, there was no doubt about the winning dish, a hair-raising jambalaya ($19) with andouille sausage, bites of chicken and tasso ham, and perfect rice.

Another winner was the Louisiana-style barbecued shrimp ($24) described as a Paul Prudhomme classic. The tuna was rather dull and the soft-shell crabs were a bit soggy. The fish of the day, on the other hand, was simple and lovely — a whole bass served with "ugly tomatoes," Creole red beans, and rice.

And then what about the dishes we didn't try? Fried catfish and hush puppies. Slap-My-Ass-and-Call-Me-Belle ribs. Cast iron-pan roast chicken. Cornmeal fried oysters over sauteed greens with Creole mustard aioli.

The helpings are large (the gumbo was a meal in itself), which means that you probably won't have room for dessert. We tried a sugar-overload mixture of chocolate ganache, mascarpone, and fresh fruit, as well as a carrot and mango cake that could have served as ballast for a fair-sized trawler. But then tastes vary so much in desserts; my neighbor scarfed it all down, going mmmm, mmmm, all the time.

As we left, the live music was just beginning, the bar was packed, and, although it was not that warm, people had spilled out into the gardens at the back.

It all spelled the summer's new hot spot to me.

June 2003

JOHN DUCK JR.'S

35 Prospect Street
Southampton
283-0311
Lunch and dinner six days. Closed Monday.

As one by one the old stores and eateries of the South Fork give way to cashmere boutiques, bling-bling shops, and Hummer emporiums, anywhere that offers down-to-earth good value becomes a find.

A family-oriented bastion of good solid fare, John Duck Jr.'s is one such. The staff at John Duck's do not drizzle raspberry coulis on the plates or flounce in with giant pepper grinders, but they serve the best duck around.

This is because the restaurant is run by the fourth generation of a family that has been serving the Long Island quackers since 1930 without changing the recipe. You get a whole half duck with apple stuffing for $19.25. The meat is moist and tender with a wonderful flavor and the skin is heaven. I'm putting this right at the front of the review, because duck is what John Duck's is all about.

The restaurant is very large, divided into a number of different rooms that presumably are opened or closed according to demand. There is a lot of wood and cheery bright green tablecloths, but cutting edge design it is not.

We were there for lunch on Valentine's Day and were seated in a light-filled sunporch liberally decorated with red hearts. Although there were plenty of couples, they were not exactly in the first flush of youth. John Duck's attracts the older crowd, big family groups, and families with small children.

This is because small children are positively welcomed, which is such a relief for parents used to seeing a film of ice form over the waitstaff when their little moppet starts acting up. Special child-sized portions of dishes are offered and drinks are served in spillproof cups.

Our waiter, noticing one child's disappointment when her sister got a cherry with her drink and she did not, went and fetched her some extra cherries without a word.

When a menu lists "clam chowder or soup of the day, bowl or cup" it does not augur well — you are probably about to get something out of a can. But in this case what turned up was a really delightful leek and potato soup. Other enjoyable appetizers were a portobello mushroom covered with fontina cheese ($6.25) and a huge bowl of really nice mussels ($6.50). A hearty plateful of fried oysters ($7.50) was also good, but the breadcrumb coating was a little heavy.

If you really don't want the duck, then the jumbo shrimp ($13.50) is highly recommended. But you might prefer to go with the unbelievably tender and tasty sautéed beef tips, which at $13.50 were a real bargain.

John Duck's coleslaw is good enough to mention and their fries are rippin'. One thing I did notice was that more attention is now paid to healthful green stuff than on my last visit. The fried oysters came with a little salad of chopped tomato and onion served in a lettuce leaf, the carrots and squash with the entrees were fresh and not overcooked, the salad with the mushroom had moved up a grade or two from iceberg, cucumber, and grated carrot.

While the rainbow sherbet was a hit with the younger members of our party, the strawberry rhubarb pie was pretty awful and should be banished from the menu.

Like the Sag Harbor five-and-dime and Bridgehampton's Candy Kitchen, John Duck Jr. is one of the places that give the South Fork its particular flavor. Long may it remain.

February 2004

LE CHEF

75 Job's Lane

Southampton

283-8581

Lunch and dinner seven days.

The lighting is soft at Le Chef, a restaurant at the foot of Job's Lane you could pass a dozen times without noticing, and the waiters are friendly. As you sink down in a comfortable seat you notice that the walls are the exact color of lobster bisque. You find you are hungry.

There are two Hamptons dining phenomena that have remained constant through my years of schlepping from Montauk to Moriches on the restaurant review trail. There is the new, trendy place that opens with an overpriced flourish at the beginning of the season only to disappear like a puff of truffle foam come fall, and there is the quiet place that finds a successful formula and sticks to it.

Le Chef is one of the latter.

Unique among South Fork restaurants, it offers a three-course prix fixe menu for $21.95 with à la carte alternatives. You can either stick to the basic menu or pay between $2 and $5 more for alternatives, the additional price being marked next to each item.

The small wine list offers a no-nonsense selection with plenty of reasonable choices. Diners lay into the hot rolls that greet them right away and the meal is half over before they register that no one has to shout to be heard, even though the place is full.

I have eaten at Le Chef a few times since 1997, which was when it was last reviewed, and the menu has stayed pretty much the same over the years. Nothing wrong with that — what works, works.

I suspect the reason for the lobster bisque walls may be that the soup is one of Le Chef's specialties, and I've never known it to disappoint. On Sunday night, the soup of the day was curried carrot — that would make a pretty wall color, too — which had a

good kick to it without in any way destroying the subtle flavor of carrot.

The crab and salmon cakes have also been on the menu since the Pliocene and cannot be too highly recommended: a perfectly balanced filling with just a little scallion for prettiness and a great crunchy exterior. The snails were a wonderful garlicky, buttery treat, too, and the mixed green salad was beautifully presented.

The ravioli du jour was lobster and Gorgonzola in a broth with mushrooms, tomatoes, and julienned carrots and squash. This was a dish that didn't work. If you mix red, blue, and yellow in the paint box you end up with brown; these ravioli had the equivalent flavor. And what was that redolent component haunting the broth? Burnt garlic was what.

But that was really the only failure of the evening. As entrees, the veal scaloppine was fine and the chicken scaloppine was really outstanding. The lamb chops, which were $5 extra, were well cooked and many. All the entrees came with unhusked rice or mashed potatoes, yellow squash, spaghetti squash, beans, and carrots.

The grilled tuna, rare as ordered, came with two interesting accompaniments, a green sauce of tomatillos and jalapeño peppers and a tomato and mango salsa. Very good. The salmon was perfectly adequate but a bit of a Plain Jane in a meal of strong flavors and lively combinations.

As everyone knows, dessert calories don't count if the dessert is part of a prix fixe meal. Le Chef has a big choice, including a fine crème caramel and a very light cheesecake. Both the lemon and the cappuccino mousse were fluffy and pleasant but strictly PG-13; they'd have been better if their flavors had been stepped up to an R.

Le Chef is a charming venue, the food is excellent and extremely good value, and the service is efficient and very accommodating. It is no accident that it has thrived for so many years.

March 2002

THE PLAZA CAFE

61 Hill Street
Southampton
283-9323
Dinner seven days.

The Plaza Cafe, tucked away in one of those mock Tudor buildings behind the Southampton Cinema, has received very good press for its imaginative, mainly seafood menu since it opened five years ago. The high-ceilinged dining room is very Hamptons — airy and understated — and is rescued from the minimalist chill of some places by the soft golden glow of its sponge-painted walls.

A quick glance at the menu and you'll find your eyes checking the right-hand side before you read the description of the dishes — the cheapest appetizer is $9 for a green salad with peaches, goat cheese, and toasted pecan nuts; the rest are $10 to $14. Entrees are $25 (chicken) to $37 (swordfish).

The wines by the glass are expensive, $9 to $15, and the special wine of the day, which perked our interest, lost it again when the price — $20 a glass — was revealed. But the wine list, with its comprehensive selection of American vintages, is fascinating, and the delicious pinot noir we chose, which came from Oregon's Willamette Valley, was fairly priced at $34.

We ordered four appetizers and found each one better than the one before. The delicate seafood sausage was nicely complemented by a lobster sauce, a little heap of finely shredded Napa cabbage, and three tiny roast potatoes. The smoked salmon Napoleon was basically smoked salmon with a little crème fraîche and a pinch of caviar with a potato chip (gaufrette sounds so much classier), but the quality was first rate.

The crab cake was immaculate — firm, good-quality meat held together by a prayer and a good crisping in the pan and served with a lovely fresh tomato and fresh corn salsa. At $11, this was worth every penny. Even better was the sauteed fresh conch, very crunchy and tasty, with a snappy black bean and mango salsa and vanilla bean sauce. On one plate or another were some perfect deep-fried basil leaves.

The adventurous mixing of tastes and textures was not always so successful when it came to the entrees, particularly in the case of the striped bass ($31), whose flavor was drowned in a cacophony of warring accompaniments: dollops of cloying sweet potato mash interspersed with lobster succotash — bits of lobster, fresh lima beans, and that baby corn you get with Chinese takeout.

The sauteed sea scallops ($27) arrived completely rare, and, as none of us thought they tasted good that way, the dish was returned. Yes, they tasted much better when they came back, but were still outshone by the really delicious polenta made from local corn, which, with local snow peas and shiitake mushrooms, was served alongside.

The Plaza Cafe's Shepherd's Pie, as fine a plateful of comfort food as you will find, substitutes a creamy mixture of lobster, shrimp, fish, local corn, and shiitake mushrooms for the traditional ground lamb, and a fine improvement it is, too.

We also tried salmon, tuna, and cod dishes. The first two were exceptionally good. The cubes of tuna, encrusted in sesame seeds, managed to be rare but not chilly in the center and well seared on the outside without burning the sesame seeds. It was accompanied by appropriately Japanese-inspired cellophane noodles, cucumber salad, and ginger and soy sauce vinaigrette.

The wild salmon had that salmon flavor you remember from childhood. In this case the accompanying mixture of haricots verts, red potatoes, shallots, and frisée with a sharp, mustardy vinaigrette was a perfect complement. The best thing about the cod, a daily special of a very small, rather dull piece of bread-crumbed fish, was the mashed potatoes under it.

The Plaza Cafe is a family affair, with Douglas Gulija in the kitchen, his wife, Andrea, taking care of the front of the house, and his mother making the desserts, which include crème brûlée and many different sorbets and ice creams.

We tried a subtle, not-too-sweet pear crisp with an intense raspberry sorbet and, served with a lovely ginger ice cream, a strawberry and peach crumble.

While the food is very good at the Plaza Cafe, the rather tense, almost martial atmosphere of the dining room did not make us feel like lingering.

September 2002

RED/BAR BRASSERIE

210 Hampton Road

Southampton

283-0704

Dinner six days May and June. Closed Tuesday.
Dinner seven days July and August.

As neatly as a KitKat bar, humanity can be divided into, say, cat lovers and dog lovers, or night owls and early birds, or those who think "Titanic" and "Gladiator" were good movies and the enlightened rest.

When stress and anxiety come along, the division is between those who lose their appetites and those who eat. While the former have been staying home recently, the latter have been dining out, chowing their way through the menu until the last profiterole has disappeared.

But food alone doesn't always cut it for anxiety quelling. What one needs as well as good food are old friends around the table in attractive and comfortable surroundings. Last weekend Red/Bar in Southampton, which has a branch on Manhattan's Upper East Side, came up trumps on all points.

The restaurant is in a rather unattractive house set back from Hampton Road, but inside, from the cozy speakeasy bar on in, it is all charm. The large dining room is surrounded by multipaned sets of windows on three sides, with large glass candleholders between each block of windows. More candles flicker on the well-spaced tables and the points of light are reflected wherever you look. It is definitely one of the prettiest dining spaces in the Hamptons.

Off-season is the time to dine there, because that way you can sidestep the restaurant's only drawback — when it is full it is extremely noisy. One of our reviewing crew was there in August and her dinner partner had to shout to be heard; the guests on the other side of the table might as well have been in Vermont for all the communication she had with them.

The carefully balanced menu is enlivened by a good choice of daily specials, and the wine list offers an interesting selection of wines by the glass, most $7 or $8. Prices are Hamptons upper end:

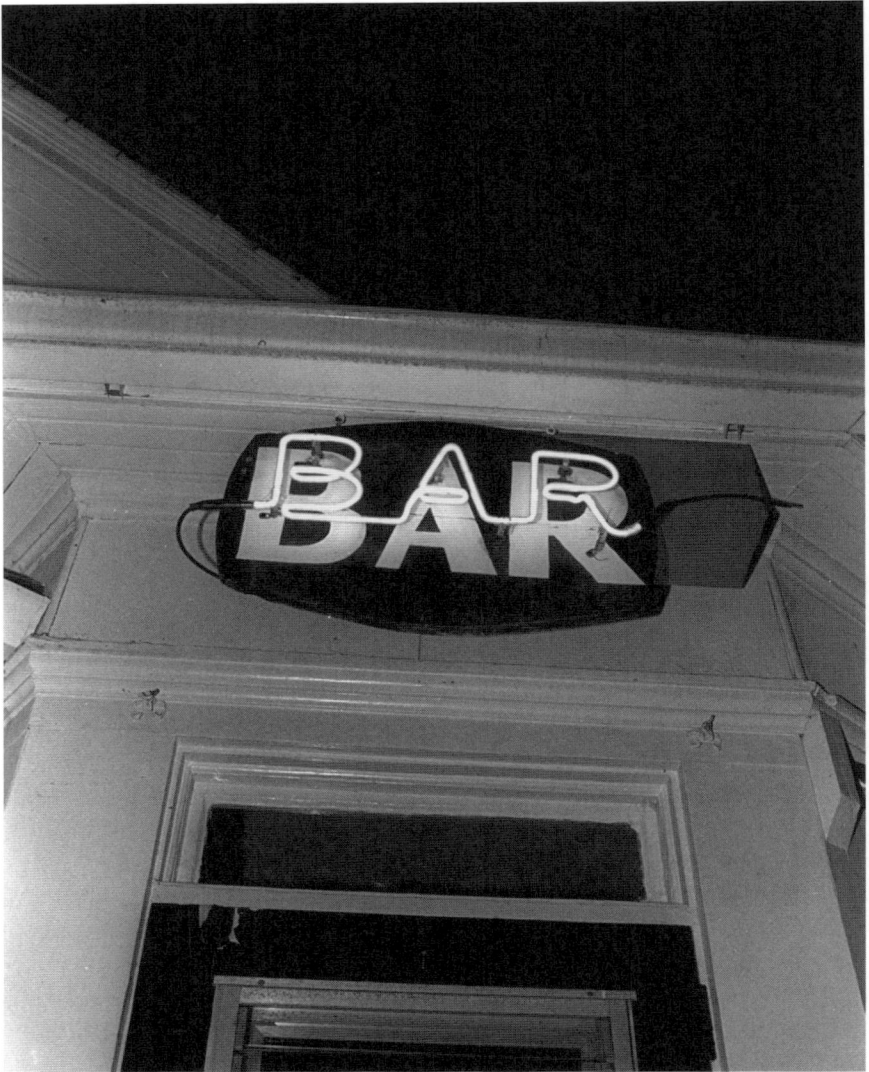

appetizers are $7 to $14; entrees $15 for an upscale burger to $35 for dry-aged strip steak.

The crab salad was voted the winning appetizer. It was turned out on the plate like a child's sandcastle, with a layer of crab topping a layer of avocado salad and accompanied by a tide of spirited pink grapefruit sauce.

I had to swap my dish of shrimp ceviche, which I had been eagerly anticipating, for my neighbor's salad. I have to recuse myself when it comes to dishes heavy with cilantro — I'll knock back tripe or pig's trotters, blood sausage or jellied eels with the best, but to me cilantro smells and tastes like soap.

Anyway, my dining partner loved it. She made embarrassing cooing noises over it, in fact, so I'll take her word that it was good.

What I received in return was a plate of paper-thin prosciutto and black figs, their red centers glowing like garnets. It conjured up the Mediterranean and seemed an appropriate dish for the last days of an Indian summer of poignant perfection.

The baby spinach and beet salad with fresh goat cheese was of exemplary freshness, with a lovely sherry walnut vinaigrette, though both the beets and the cheese were a little too firm.

The service was of the best kind; one was barely aware of it. Dishes and drinks came and went in perfect order.

A $32 grilled filet mignon with mashed potatoes and big, fat asparagus was not an exciting dish. Nothing wrong with it, just not very inspiring.

The striped bass, on the other hand, was a dream. Pan-roasted in a crisp crust of hazelnut crumbs, its redolent pan juices swirling around the most delicious herbed mashed potatoes, it was surrounded by a ring of crisp French beans and slivers of fresh artichoke (not those nasty things from the can).

The roast duck was a tender, comforting dish but its skin was not crisp and the mango-ginger sauce was wimpy and bland. A B-minus for that, but certainly an A for the one pasta dish on the menu ($19), a simple dish of spaghettini with broccoli rabe, tomato, garlic, and crushed red pepper that was clean and light, with every flavor sparklingly clear.

And an A-plus for the two desserts we tried: a chocolate souffle cake and a featherlight dream of a raspberry financier.

Like a number of East End restaurants, Red/Bar has a split personality. In high season the place is packed with logo-bearing 30-year-olds, and noise ricochets like gunfire. When the calm of autumn comes, the trendy young things with the loud voices hightail it to the city, leaving the dining room to quieter diners. Enjoy it while the going's good.

November 2001

SANT AMBROEUS

30 Main Street

Southampton

283-1233

Lunch and dinner seven days. Coffee bar from 10 AM. Seasonal.

Sant Ambroeus appears to be an elegant patisserie on Main Street in Southampton. There is practically no indication that hidden behind it is a small Art Deco Italian restaurant with the atmosphere of a private supper club, so sure of its clientele that on Saturday it was serving a fresh truffle appetizer at $55.

It is so discreet it could have been an elegant speakeasy patronized by Daisy and Tom Buchanan (who, "The Great Gatsby" tells us, lived just down the road), a fancy borne out by the diners, many of whom could have been scions of West Egg.

The restaurant is divided into two intimate carpeted dining rooms with banquettes, booths, a few freestanding tables, and low lighting. Even when every table is taken, the noise level is pleasantly subdued.

A first glance at the menu is heart-stopping — arugula salad for $18, asparagus vinaigrette, $14.50, veal chop, $36 — but don't be daunted; with judicious ordering you can eat for under $50 a head with wine (even with wines by the glass starting at $8). And if it does cost more, you will probably agree that it was worth it, because the food is very good indeed.

The menu is divided into cold plates; a choice of four salads, carpaccio, first course, homemade pasta, risotto; second course, fish and grilled food, which is rather confusing. While "second course" is meat dishes, "first course" is pasta dishes, priced similarly to the "homemade pastas."

Considering it was a cold November night, with the village outside looking about as populous as the Gobi Desert, there was an impressive number of specials, including those pricey black or white truffle dishes. A glance at the neighboring table told us that a special appetizer of a one-pound-lobster salad looked worth the $20 asked.

Carpaccio is obviously a signature dish at Sant Ambroeus, being served in three different ways ($20 to $22), and the menu also offers a salmon version, bresaola (air-dried beef), prosciutto, magatello (thinly sliced cold veal), and smoked salmon.

The restaurant serves the best quality bread and provides a small plate of choux pastry cheese puffs to open the appetite; service was brisk, with occasional weak spots.

Trying to keep within budget we ordered two mixed salads ($9.50 each) and a plate of bresaola ($16.50) for the four of us. Our waitress (who was maybe the head honcho helping out) divided the finely chopped salads onto four plates without being asked. Not only was each helping more than adequate in size, it was exceptionally good, as was the large plateful of the delicate beef.

It would seem a good idea to start with something light or to share a salad as we did, because the second course dishes we tried were gorgeously calorific — no holding back on the butter and cream here. It seemed appropriate to try the homemade pasta, and merely a glance at the ricotta ravioli with butter and sage ($20) put on a couple of pounds. But, from the rich sauce down to the deep-fried fresh sage-leaf garnish, the dish was worth every ounce.

Almost as good was the tagliatelle with fresh and smoked salmon; lovely buttery pasta, though maybe a tad salty. The serving of glistening risotto didn't look very big, but halfway through, good though it was (and rare though it is to find good risotto around here), I had to give up and take the rest home. It tasted even better the next day.

We also tried a classic veal piccatine in a white wine sauce ($34) which was all that could be wished for, with a carefully prepared accompaniment of perfect mashed potatoes and lightly steamed adolescent garden vegetables.

As the trek through the patisserie, with its delightful trompe l'oeil mural, will show you, the desserts at Sant Ambroeus are something else. There are dozens of cakes and pastries, all decorated as if they were entries in the Wedding Cake Bake-Off of the Year. Just the one (large) slice of profiterole cake we tried among the four of us — chocolate mousse, choux pastry, Chantilly crème, cake moistened with coffee — almost defeated us.

After a heavy meal, one of the gelati (coffee with a cup of hot espresso or vanilla with hot chocolate maybe) might have been a better choice. As a point of interest, Sant Ambroeus is famous for its panettone, made by a master baker imported from Italy.

The hometown of Sant Ambroeus is Milan, and it also has a branch in Manhattan. Of the latter, the new Zagat writes, "Recherche East Side Northern Italian cafe patronized by a cell-phone equipped older crowd and known for its earthy entrees, heavenly desserts, and stiff tabs; aficionados advise 'take the gelati and run.'"

Yes, but they have a choice among more good restaurants there. While the "stiff tab" bit is certainly true, careful ordering will get you a fine meal and still leave you with a few pennies for the bus fare home.

November 2000

75 MAIN

75 Main Street
Southampton
283-7575
Breakfast, lunch, and dinner seven days.

When we drove past 75 Main in Southampton on Saturday night, the joint was jumping, but Sunday night the whole town seemed to have shut down and it was very quiet.

Show me a ghost town in New Mexico, with the dust of generations seeping over the doorsills and the wind howling through the broken windows, and show me Southampton on a cold Sunday night in April and there's no prize for guessing which one is the more depressing.

75 Main obviously knows this and so, since moving to a livelier town is probably not in the cards, it has instigated a Sunday tea dance. A small dance floor was cleared at one end of the dining room and a flashing red light installed, and as we trooped through the door we were welcomed by the rhythmic thump of disco music.

It was a rhythmic thump that accompanied our meal until we were the last people in the place, even though no one at all danced while we were there.

So 75 Main comes across as a bit of a chameleon, its restrained, beautifully lighted dining room contrasting with an oversized bar decorated with funky, glitter-covered artwork; the flashing red disco light and thumping disco music is somewhat at odds with one of the best wine lists on the East End.

More on that wine list — not only were there great variety and interesting choices among the more expensive wines, but the same applied to the large selection of inexpensive wines. We tried two reds, a Crozes Hermitage at $28 that everyone found a bit thin and a universally liked Liberty cabernet from the Napa Valley at $26.

Having secured a table as far away from the music as possible, our evening began well with an attentive waiter, excellent chewy bread, and a plateful of tasty snacks to open the appetite. Thereafter the service was slow, considering there was only one other table occupied.

The menu is well-balanced, though with few surprises, and the prices are the equivalent of those at most high-end Hamptons places: $7 to $12 for appetizers and $19 to $27 for entrees, the latter being for a Black Angus sirloin steak that would have been over $30 in many places.

We started with three appetizers among five of us, all of which were fresh and interesting. The vegetable spring roll was crisp and light with a lively sauce of apple cider and basil to dip it in. The spicy peanut shrimp were very good though the zippy little hummock of Oriental greens they were balanced on was even better.

When the Asian vegetable salad was delivered, a wonderful blast of fresh ginger suffused the whole table. The salad was a hit, including the little pieces of crisp taro that were included.

Other appetizers included the ubiquitous fried calamari, mussels in saffron broth, a beet and arugula salad with pecans and a little cheese, tuna carpaccio, and, which sounded particularly nice, a warm duck salad with frisée, bacon, and caramelized onions.

The one surprise among the entrees was white tuna ($28), usually seen only in sushi bars. It was cooked in a sesame crust and served with avocado mashed potatoes and pickled ginger. It was interesting, both delicious and a little disconcerting. The first bite tasted like a delicate white fish, but by the third or fourth bite you had become aware of how rich it was and how that ginger was needed to cut the fattiness.

A nicely cooked duck breast ($25) was served on a bed of very oversalted spinach with some wild-rice cakes that were dry and dull and a lively pear and mango chutney that just managed to rescue the dish. Pan-seared scallops ($25) were more simmered than seared but otherwise perfectly okay, though the cabbage that accompanied them didn't make anyone leap up and shout hallelujah!

One of the most inexpensive entrees, local fluke ($20), turned out to be the best dish we tried — crisp and gratinéed on the outside and full of flavor, it raised the lowly fluke to a higher level. And the cheapest entree, the rosemary flavored chicken

breast ($19), was also tender and full of flavor (though the polenta was dry and stodgy).

High marks for the two desserts we tried, a rich petit pot au chocolat smothered in a whipped white chocolate cream and a classic apple turnover.

April 2003

SHIPPY'S PUMPERNICKELS

36 Windmill Lane
Southampton
283-0007
Lunch Monday through Saturday. Dinner seven days.

I don't know if Shippy's Pumpernickels is much of a magnet on a hot summer night, but when the temperature plummets and the sound of the snowplow is heard in the land then it is just the place you want to go.

Hearty stews, heavy on protein and carbohydrates, huge portions of comfort food, steaks on sizzling platters, lots of wursts and other German specialties — this is old-fashioned, feel-good fare.

If you are a vegetarian, walk on by.

The decor matches the menu. It's dim and warm and gemütlich and publike — dark wood, booths, and faux Tiffany lamps. You might expect Tyrolean mountain scenes but the walls are covered with murals of the Shinnecock Hills Golf Club, which adds some quirky appeal.

And as it is the holiday season, Shippy's was laden with little model houses, a flashing Christmas tree, and a windowful of inebriated snowmen. That, and the very friendly service for which Shippy's is known, is guaranteed to put even the most entrenched bah-humbugger in a cheerful mood.

The focus at Shippy's is definitely on the entrees. Because they come with a choice of a (very generic) soup or salad, I suspect that most customers pass over the other appetizers, which are not very exciting — marinated herring, chopped liver, baked clams, onion rings, shrimp cocktail, all between $5.25 and $9.50. You can, however, get clams and oysters on the half shell and also a sliced tongue and onion salad that you won't find elsewhere.

Wines by the glass are reasonable but somehow a dark beer on tap seems the way to go.

The first list of entrees are all German specialties. There's a wiener schnitzel that overlaps the plate like a down comforter ($22.95) and a delicious, if slightly overwhelming, dish called beef rouladen ($21.95), which is thinly rolled strips of beef filled with

pickles, onions, and bacon served with gravy and mashed potatoes.

If you are a sausage lover, you can't go wrong with bratwurst, knockwurst, or weisswurst, all served with sauerkraut and mashed potatoes ($18.95), or *kassler rippchen* ($20.95), which is not the fateful nemesis from "The Usual Suspects" but a smoked pork chop. Wiener rostbraten is a pounded Black Angus steak sauteed with onions ($24.95).

Shippy's excels at pork chops, which they also serve on the bone, beaten thin and breaded. The other evening, Hungarian goulash was one of the specials. A good, spicy choice for a cold evening, it was served over butterfly pasta.

Although there are a certain number of fish dishes, and there are always fresh fish choices among the daily specials, this is basically a meat-and-potatoes restaurant. The sirloin steak is excellent though the veal cordon bleu is a little over-rich. On a recent night, when we tried the very good rack of lamb ($25.95), it turned out to be no fewer than nine chops.

The list of desserts is all you need to know — Bavarian chocolate cream pie, chocolate fudge cake, apple strudel, Black Forest cake, cheesecake, carrot cake, and ice cream sundaes.

Yes, it's an old-fashioned place, and sometimes that is exactly what you need.

December 2003

Q — A THAI BISTRO

129 Noyac Road

North Sea

204-0007

For my money, there can't be too many Thai restaurants. So it was good news to hear that a new one had opened in North Sea. Particularly good news for those who live in that part of the world, because if you are coming from points east and taking Noyac Road I'll swear a trip to Nova Scotia is shorter.

Q's dining room is small and cute, with a comfortable, friendly feel and good acoustics, and there is a small and cute bar. The two rooms are in a small and cute white building. All in all, very cute.

There is a nice selection of alien beers and wines by the glass, though the list is not particularly cheap. And do not expect Ninth Avenue Thai food prices on the menu either.

To start a meal, the bang bang shrimp are a good choice. Marinated, grilled, and full of flavor, they are served with an interesting mint and peanut dipping sauce. The grilled beef salad, served over a salad of mixed greens and pan roasted rice, was terrific and is highly recommended. Dump the dumplings, however; the stuffing was good but the casings were completely mushy. All the dishes are very nicely presented.

The best entree we tried was a daily special, a wonderful spicy jumbo shrimp with noodles and the most delicious sauce. It was served with Chinese green beans that were a good foot in length. When you dream of Thai flavors, this is the kind of dish you have in mind; its memory stored close to the brain's pleasure center.

But the whole red snapper in a coconut curry sauce with Thai herbs was almost as good. You can also choose to have the snapper in a hot, hot garlic sauce. We passed on the traditional Pad Thai, that noodle, shrimp, bean sprout, and peanut dish that is a favorite with everyone who tries it, and went instead for "drunken noodles," a richer, darker noodle dish with beef, garlic, and red peppers. Once again, it was very good.

The Q chicken was a slight disappointment because the peanut sauce had in no way penetrated the breast's rubbery bounce. When genetic engineering is perfected, perhaps chickens can be encouraged to grow thigh meat all over.

Rice is served in attractive woven baskets. When you take the lid off, though, the rice is in plastic bags. Would you find a plastic bag inside your basket in Nakhon Ratchasima? I think not. I'm sure the baskets are hell to clean up, but plastic bags spoil the mood. Aesthetics aside, the rice was perfect.

There are a number of conventional desserts, but by the end of the meal you are so much in the Thai mood that the thought of chocolate cake brings a shudder. Had there been some mango and sticky rice it would have been different.

Q is a charming spot. We had a good time, could have a conversation without shouting, and thoroughly enjoyed our meal. The food was about 75 percent excellent and 25 percent pretty good. The flavors could be a little sharper, a little cleaner, and the prices could be a little lower.

October 2002

WITCH'S ROCK RESTAURANT

450 County Road 39
Southampton
259-8999
Dinner Thursday through Sunday.

Witch's Rock is a famous surfing spot in Costa Rica. While it will be a cold day in hell before I mount a surfboard, I will happily surf my Honda to Witch's Rock in Southampton any time, after having had a really terrific meal there the other night.

Reviewing East End restaurants year after year, it is wonderful when you get taken by surprise. There are the funny surprises, like the time a waiter, all unaware, crossed the room bearing a bread basket at shoulder height that had somehow caught fire, and the satisfying surprises, such as finding a charming restaurant with excellent food where you expected nothing.

We had low expectations because Witch's Rock is in an odd place, next to a motel right beside the depressing County Road 39. But inside it has a tented canvas ceiling, great lighting, and huge paintings of fruit on the walls. While being comfortable, it manages to convey the feeling of a beach cafe.

And, bliss, a menu that lists *pulpo seductor* and ceviche instead of 14 pastas and "sinful warm chocolate cake."

Witch's Rock has a small but adequate wine list with nearly every bottle at an affordable price. Menu prices are slightly hard to assess because many of the appetizers — that octopus for example — are big enough for entrees.

They start with a Costa Rican white bean soup for $5.50. There are small salads and large salads, and appetizers are between $7.50 and $12.50. Half the entrees are under $20, the rest just above, with a 10-ounce lobster tail with mixed vegetables being the most expensive dish at $25.

Service was excellent, attentive without being bothersome, hot rolls delivered at once, drink orders whipped to the table at double speed.

Among the appetizers we didn't try were a cream soup of lobster, fish, and shrimp, lobster bisque, and a seafood wrap. There are three different ceviches and we tried the simple whitefish one,

which our waitress recommended. It was a heady wake-up call of lime and onion and cilantro that opened the appetite and made one ready for whatever was to follow.

The *pulpo seductor*, sautéed octopus cooked with garlic, butter, and white wine, was tender and delicious. But the crown of laurels goes to the outstanding Ocean Soup, as good a fish soup (shrimp, fish, calamari, octopus, and scallops) as I have had in years.

There is a choice from among 20 different entrees, most with a Costa Rican influence but plenty that were more mainstream. We tried three Costa Rican dishes, and highly recommend them all.

Mariscada ($21) is a selection of sautéed octopus, shrimp, calamari, scallops, and different fish in a wonderful broth with a pile of rice in the center.

Arroz con Mariscos ($19.75), on the other hand, was a smooth mound of rice with the shellfish incorporated into the rice. Sounds a little similar, but they really weren't. Then there was the Costa Rican Typical Dish ($18) — rice and gallo pinto beans served with a crisp salad and slices of highly seasoned sirloin steak. We passed our plates to one another, but couldn't agree which one we liked best.

We finished our meal with a *dulce de tres leches*, three-milk pudding, cream, milk, and condensed milk with a base of saturated bread, dappled with a little fudge sauce.

Can I in all honesty recommend this? Even though we shared it among us, I was calculating the calories per spoonful, and I had a sickening feeling that had I been alone I would nonetheless have finished every mouthful.

The paramount impression of our meal was of the clarity of flavors in every dish. The chef at Witch's Rock has a masterly hand when it comes to seasoning — no one flavor overwhelmed the others yet each one made its mark and was identifiable. Although the helpings were large and some contained generous amounts of rice, we ate everything but did not feel over full.

Don't be put off by the location — Witch's Rock is a find.

May 2003

WEST OF THE CANAL

THE COOPERAGE INN

2218 Sound Avenue
Baiting Hollow
727-8994
Lunch Monday through Saturday. Dinner Monday through Sunday.

The Cooperage Inn in Baiting Hollow is a surprise, and it is not one that you would discover on your own, as it is housed in a fairly nondescript building on the far side of Riverhead.

Although Riverhead is slowly being transformed, the approach from the South Fork, through Flanders, is still depressing. Keep going through the town and you hit the infamous Old Country Road, which is cheek-by-jowl car dealerships and huge warehouse stores (including Borders, Target, Best Buy, Pottery Barn, and Home Depot for those who care). It feels as if you have crash-landed in Nassau County.

But although the stores line the road, immediately behind them is open countryside the like of which we no longer see on the South Fork, and Sound Avenue, one of the prettiest roads on the East End.

In keeping with its name, and its location in the middle of North Fork wine country, the decor at the Cooperage Inn is, well, wine-related. There are grape-covered tablecloths, grape-covered upholstery, and grape-covered curtains. The carpet has bunches of flowers. The colors are burgundy, claret, and vine-leaf green. A rustic frieze of fields and farmhouses circles the walls, as do great swaths of plastic vines and bunches of plastic grapes.

I felt the onset of a panic attack but then, after seeing that even the glass oil and vinegar containers were also bunches of grapes and finding the ladies room so full of china roosters and little embroidered cushions you could hardly turn around, I gave in and admitted that it was fun and really rather appealing.

And I wish that any number of noisy places on the South Fork would use carpet and acoustic tiles.

The Cooperage Inn offers no fewer than 20 wines by the glass, nearly all for $6. The service is super efficient — our drinks, a selection of different rolls and breads, and our first course arrived like lightning. Presentation is delightful and I'm happy to report that the elegant square white dishes have no grapes on them.

Appetizers at lunchtime start at $5 for soup and include toasted cheese ravioli ($6.50), baked clams ($7.50), mussels ($8.50), and crab cakes ($7.50).

Salads are taken seriously. The house salad includes apples, mandarin oranges, toasted almonds, and raisins. There is a blackened shrimp and chicken salad with roasted peppers, a shrimp salad with spinach, Gorgonzola, mushrooms, bacon, and candied pecans, and a crusted calamari salad.

Pastas, between $10.50 and $13.50, include chicken, shrimp, sweet and hot sausage with zucchini and yellow squash with fusilli or a seafood pasta with shrimp, mussels, scallops, lobsters, wild mushrooms, and spinach in a pesto sauce.

Entrees include flounder and salmon, chicken and veal dishes, baby back ribs ($10.75), meat loaf, chicken pot pie ($10.50), and pork chop with garlic mashed potatoes, also $10.50.

The dinner menu has similar prices but a few additions. Sunday brunch offers a buffet with an enormous selection of dishes and a complimentary mimosa or Bloody Mary for $21.95.

I've had a couple of really lousy bowls of clam chowder recently, but when I tasted the Cooperage Inn's clam chowder with seasonal vegetables I was reminded just how wonderful it should be.

But let me tell you about the crabmeat and shrimp bisque ($5) — this is soup; this is what you dream of when you are stranded on that desert island and say to yourself, "I'd sell my soul for a bowl of seafood bisque." Hey, it's even good enough to make a special trip to Riverhead.

For $7.50 you get two exemplary crab cakes, crisp and not weighed down with unnecessary filling, with corn and tomato salsa and lemon caper sauce.

And of course there are daily specials. On the day we were there they included a truly impressive quail salad for $12 or so. Two whole quail cut in halves were served with a scoop of crabmeat over a salad of frisée with tart slices of black plum and toasted walnuts. It was an imaginative and wholly successful dish served at a reasonable price.

A rather more conventional dish, though still great value at $12.50, is the Veal Tuscano, served with prosciutto, roasted red peppers, artichoke hearts, and spinach in a hearty port wine sauce with mashed potatoes. Definitely a guy dish.

Another daily special was a very good blackened catfish ($12.50) with various vegetables and — a good idea, here — steak fries served in a separate dish.

Desserts are made on the premises and include a coconut pie — very fluffy and different from the usual gluey mess you get — and a nice fruit crumble.

About the only complaint we had was with the music, an endless tinkling piano monotonously burbling without any change of style from Paul McCartney to "Carmen" to Bach's "Sheep May Safely Graze" to Neil Diamond to that old favorite, the Taco Bell Canon. Beyond Awful.

October 2003

THE OLD BARGE

75 Old Main Road

Southold

765-4700

Lunch and dinner seven days.

On the South Fork, restaurants right on the water are a rare plea-sure; on the North Fork, every cove and creek seems to have a place to sit and look at the water, the boats, and the occasional great blue heron while eating clams on the half shell with a cold beer.

On Sunday, with perfect weather at last, I took the ferries across to Greenport, which is a pleasure in itself, turned left, and upon reaching Hashamomuck Pond turned onto a dirt road, rather grandly called Old Main Road, where there were no fewer than three restaurants perched on the edge of Southold Bay.

While there are a few notable exceptions, most of these waterside places have fairly simple menus and reasonable prices. The Old Barge is one such. Their wine list, for example, offers over a dozen of both red and white wines, nearly all local. All of the whites were under $28 and all of the reds were under $30, with one lone bottle hitting $30.

For lunch on a sunny day, obviously the deck is the place to sit, but the Old Barge also has a large and attractive dining room with wonderful views across to Shelter Island. The theme is nauti-cal, with a vengeance — the bar is the Upper Deck, the dining room is festooned with fishing nets and plaster crabs and lobsters, and other seafaring drollery abounds.

The service, on the deck at least, was of the friendly, helpful, thumb-in-the-soup, high-schooler-working-on-the-weekend variety.

Appetizers are between $5.95 and $7.95, chowders are $2.95 for a mug or $4.95 for a bowl. Salads start at $4.25 for a plain green salad and rise to $8.95 for a chef's salad. A cold lobster plat-ter with a half lobster, shrimp, and crab legs is $13.95.

There is a good selection of hot sandwiches and burgers, steak, and chicken dishes (all under $20) and at least a dozen seafood dishes, from crab cakes to the daily fish special. Most of the entrees come with a large salad.

As they seemed rather too substantial for lunch, we did not try any of the Old Barge's pasta entrees, but they include shrimp and scampi Provençal, seafood fra diavolo, and penne à la vodka.

The fried calamari got a winning vote — they were legion, they were tender, and the breadcrumb coating was very light. But even better than the calamari were the mussels, which were huge and perfectly cooked in a nice garlic and white wine broth.

We will pass over the New England and Manhattan clam chowders in silence, hoping they will die of humiliation and be reincarnated as a higher form of soup.

Simple is what the Old Barge does well. A fillet of bass served over salad greens was all that could be asked. The flavor of the salmon cakes, on the other hand, had been ruined by the inclusion of what appeared to be chopped dill pickles.

We do recommend the stuffed shrimp scampi ($18.95) which, while one of the more expensive dishes and very rich and buttery, was certainly delicious. Which reminded us that we were not served any bread, because we needed something to dunk in the juice.

There is a large selection of desserts, very prettily presented. They included the ubiquitous flourless chocolate cake you find everywhere, which is a real turn-on for those people whose idea of heaven is eating chocolate Spackle. Then there was a three-berry pie, obviously made on the premises, which was so-so.

The Old Barge is the ideal place to unwind and relax and enjoy the beauty of this land of bays and Bacchus, offering as it does a perfect view and the chance to sample different North Fork wines at reasonable prices. When it comes to the menu, the prices are right and simple dishes are the way to go.

September 2003

SULTAN'S KITCHEN
1077 Old Country Road
Riverhead
369-9766
Open 11 AM to 10 PM daily. Closed Mondays in the winter.
Reservations on weekends.

Apple tea served in a gold-rimmed glass: It's a wonderful aromatic discovery, but you'll have to go to Riverhead to try it.

On the other hand, since everyone has to go to Riverhead some time or other, the knowledge that there is an inexpensive and interesting Turkish restaurant within easy reach might make the trip bearable.

I say that because most of us find ourselves in Riverhead for the wrong reasons. We are there not to visit the fine aquarium or explore the town's pleasant riverfront, we are stuck in the endless limbo of jury duty or we are waiting on line at the county offices or — get out the garlic and the silver bullets — being reduced to tears at the DMV.

You would never stop at Sultan's Kitchen unless you had been told about it. It is just past the traffic island on Old Country Road, near Dunkin' Donuts, a stone's throw from AID Auto Parts, and next door to Lobster Wok. The exterior is beyond ugly. The interior is endearingly decorated with tinsel, artificial flowers, lots of red, tchotchkes of all kinds, and some out-of-place abstract art.

The Turkish waitresses, some of whom are still having language difficulties, are unfailingly sweet and helpful. They are happy to explain to the ignorant the meaning of *sigara boregi* (pastry stuffed with feta and fresh parsley), *mercimek corbasi* (red lentil soup), or *arnavut cigeri* (deep-fried breaded liver with herbs and seasonings).

As Turkish beer tastes depressingly like Budweiser, it is far better to drink the apple tea. A clear golden yellow, it bears the same relationship to hot apple cider as paté de foie gras does to Spam.

The first and main thing to mention about the food at Sultan's Kitchen is that everything seems to be made on the premises.

Until I tasted their stuffed grape leaves, *yaprak sarma*, I had always believed they were one of the world's most dispiriting and nasty foods. It was with considerable surprise that I learned the leaves don't have to be bitter and fibrous and the filling doesn't have to be slimy and tasteless. These leaves were tissue-thin and the filling of rice and pine nuts was seasoned with a mysterious spice, like smoky cardamom.

Soups are $3, appetizers $3.50 to $4.75, and entrees $7.95 to $11.95, which includes a salad. There are eight Turkish pizzas, $6.50 to $7.95. The obviously made-that-minute chopped salad of lightly dressed tomatoes, peppers, scallions, cilantro, and parsley gave us a good feeling for what was to follow.

Since you are going to get a salad anyway, the way to go for appetizers would be to order a mixture. Although we were three adults and two children, we were advised against ordering the $16.95 large portion, and, indeed, the $8.95 small portion was more than enough for all..

It included the stuffed grape leaves and a bowl of baba ganush, a typical Turkish dish of pureed char-grilled eggplant, sesame oil, garlic, lemon, and mayonnaise. Equally good and original was the eggplant salad, *patlican salatasi*, pureed eggplant mixed with finely chopped peppers, scallions, parsley, tomatoes, and lemon juice.

The dishes were extremely simple, fresh, and delicately seasoned — a small dish of white kidney beans tossed with lemon and olive oil, for instance, and a Russian salad of diced potatoes and vegetables in mayonnaise. They were greatly enhanced by round loaves of rich, chewy bread.

Of the two winning entrees, one was a kebab of amazingly tender marinated lamb with pearl onions and mushrooms served with rice and bulgur wheat. The other was *iskendar kebab*, an eye-opening concoction of rice topped with cubes of fried bread and thin slices of spit-roasted lamb and covered with a fresh tomato sauce and yogurt. I tell you, it was terrific.

The *adana kebab* — patties of hand-chopped lamb shaped on skewers — was hotly spicy and good, but outshone by the others. The children shared an enormous falafel sandwich, each half arriving wrapped in silvery paper like a Christmas gift. Inside, the crunchy falafel, tomato, lettuce, and such were wrapped in unleavened pita bread. Very good.

Desserts revealed that Turks have a sweet tooth. We tried a creamy rice pudding, sherbet, and some little honey-soaked doughnuts, all good but very sugary.

So there you have it, a charming Turkish restaurant, with low prices and interesting food, hidden away in Riverhead's commercial wasteland of fast food stops and car dealerships. Make a note of it. You never know when the next jury duty summons is going to pop through your letter box.

February 2003

TIERRA MAR

231 Dune Road
Westhampton Beach
288-2700
Lunch and dinner seven days. Sunday brunch.

One of the tenets of garden design is that a beautiful view is doubly appreciated if a visitor comes upon it unawares — round a corner, through a gap in a wall, framed by a rose-covered arch – the impression it makes will be memorable.

Tierra Mar in Westhampton Beach is not particularly easy to find and not very inspiring to look at once you get there. You cross a small bridge over a narrow arm of Moriches Bay to be met by a wall of anonymous buildings. There's nothing to suggest that the ocean is anywhere near.

The lobby, which the restaurant shares with the Bath and Tennis Hotel, leads to a series of steps going up — and up — and... Pow! There in front of you, framed by a room of Gatsbyesque splendor, is the ocean.

I'd take this winter view of trawlers, green sea, and snow-covered dunes over the summer one, which would inevitably contain a few meaty, overcooked sunbathers.

The soaring dining room, with its white columns, crystal chandelier, and 15-foot waterfalls of swagged blue-and-white-striped wall hangings, is luminously bright. The fabric is slightly faded, which somehow adds to the room's hedonistic pre-Depression aura.

The chef at Tierra Mar is Todd Jacobs, whom East Enders may remember from the American Hotel in Sag Harbor, where he cooked for seven years. And, like the American Hotel, Tierra Mar has a seriously heavy-duty wine list, which has been seven years in the building. Its listing of premier cru Cordeaux drew an awed and respectful silence.

But we were there for Sunday brunch, and a glass of the house merlot did very nicely, thank you. The brunch costs $16.95, includes an appetizer buffet and your choice from among 16 entrees, and is a bargain.

The appetizers when we were there, all of which were excellent, included a tomato and mozzarella salad, three different green salads, Chinese sesame noodles with snow peas, house-cured smoked salmon with dill cream, salamis and pepperonis, carrot salad with roast vegetables, and the best fresh pineapple.

Among the entrees are charbroiled salmon, seafood crepes with spinach hollandaise, or a mixed grill of local fish. For a couple of dollars more you can have a dozen oysters, warm lobster salad, or an Angus sirloin steak.

Brunch staples such as waffles and Hatfield ham, eggs Benedict, steak and poached eggs, French toast and Canadian bacon, and a club sandwich abound, but, apart from the younger members of our party, who had fresh fruit pancakes with particularly nice sausages, we opted to choose something more adventurous.

The winner was a divine shellfish bourride, whose broth, aromatic with fennel and saffron, contained mussels, scallops, whitefish, some winter greens, and a piece of perfectly cooked salmon which had obviously been added just at the end of the preparation. Everything was perfect except for a couple of dry and taste-less shrimp.

While the tempura batter on the crab cake entree was a little heavy, the filling was exemplary. It was balanced on a bed of rice noodles and surrounded by little orange cedillas of concentrated carrot puree.

And then there was this great pasta — a quarter of a crisp, moist, rosemary-roasted chicken teetering on a big bowl of penne with green beans, broccoli rabe, kale, red peppers, yellow squash, carrots, garlic, and zucchini.

Sound good? It was.

Dessert isn't included in the prix fixe, but I couldn't help noticing other diners sneaking back to the appetizer buffet to fin-ish off the fresh fruit, particularly that wonderful pineapple, which had disappeared by the time we caught on and did the same ourselves.

February 2001

WHITE TRUFFLE INN

578 Montauk Highway
East Moriches
874-0757
Lunch and dinner Wednesday through Sunday all summer.

Crocuses have flowered, skunk cabbage is pushing up all over, and daffodils, maybe unwisely, are all poised for action. It is no time to be huddled by the fire, it is time to be out and about.

What I'm getting around to, in my discursive way, is that I have a restaurant to recommend, but to get there you have to go to East Moriches. Though I might not recommend driving there on a Saturday evening in August, the White Truffle Inn is well worth the painless drive at this time of year.

The restaurant is in one of those charming Addams family mansions that liven up Long Island's villages. It has one large dining room and a smaller dining area on the sunporch by the front door. This is where we ate on Sunday, and a more agreeable place would be hard to find: all white wicker armchairs, antique white linen tablecloths, pre-Raphaelite paintings, pink glass lamps, and restrained chintz.

The lunch menu is small but supplemented by an equal number of specials. The prices, particularly considering the quality of the food, are very reasonable — superlative lamb chops in a merlot reduction sauce, for example, were $16.95.

The lamb chops came with memorable roast potatoes that had been sliced so that they could absorb the sauce, and the combined aromas of rosemary and rich wine sauce would have opened the appetite of a stone.

The service is friendly and obliging. Although there is no children's menu, we were offered a choice between spaghetti and chicken fingers for our two young diners (who nonetheless chose mussels), and when they asked for ice cream for dessert, the chef created a dish of chocolate ice cream, hot fudge sauce, and whipped cream just for them.

The White Truffle Inn is one of those places, and wise they are, that get you in a good mood with little details: iced curls of butter brought to the table beneath a silver dome, hot rolls, lemon

and orange slices in the iced water, and beautiful presentation throughout.

The fat mussels in a pungent white wine, parsley, and garlic broth that the children ate arrived in a lovely bowl and were served on Italian floral latticework plates. There were two salads of the day, one being mache with mussels and shrimp. The other — whole leaves of radicchio and endive sprinkled with roast walnuts, crumbs of Gorgonzola, and thin slices of Anjou pear topped with a raspberry vinaigrette dressing — was a breath of spring.

The regular menu features brie baked in puff pastry; we went for a daily special, which was the same dish with caramelized apple added. In this case, more was less, because the apple made it a bit too much like dessert — go with the original. Pastry of one kind or another figures in a number of dishes and is obviously one of the chef's strong suits.

The most expensive appetizer listed was $12.95, and this was not only the best but also quite large enough for an entree. It was a layered construction of portobello mushroom, shrimp, and prosciutto, anchored in place by mozzarella and served with home-made salsa and a little salad with balsamic dressing. It sounds a bit heavy, but it wasn't. It was fabulous.

Two large pieces of seared tuna served à la Niçoise with black olives, tomatoes, and garlic over a bed of arugula is a good choice for those who have been warned that amazing desserts lie ahead. Cannelloni with a delicate veal, spinach, and tomato filling was an excellent value at $10.95.

The desserts served at the White Truffle Inn are the sort you dream about when you spend six months on the tundra living in a tent and eating moss fritters. They are desserts as they should be, calorific and full of all the good, fattening things of life and not for dieters. But they are nonetheless featherlight and do not leave you feeling as if you couldn't eat for a month.

Perhaps the best was a fresh fruit Napoleon with amazing mille-feuille pastry. Close behind it came a small sugar concerto that modestly called itself a peach cake but was a layered combination of baked peaches, fresh cream, caramel, liquor-soaked sponge cake, puff pastry, crème anglaise, crumbled fragments of meringue, and little dabs of kiwi jelly.

We also tried a very pretty caramel roll covered in chocolate and served with butter pecan ice cream. Nice though it was, it was drowned out by the two prima donnas in the previous paragraph.

The White Truffle Inn is owned by a husband and wife chef team, Osvaldo and Nohemi Cuenca. It is a real find.

February 2002

MAP

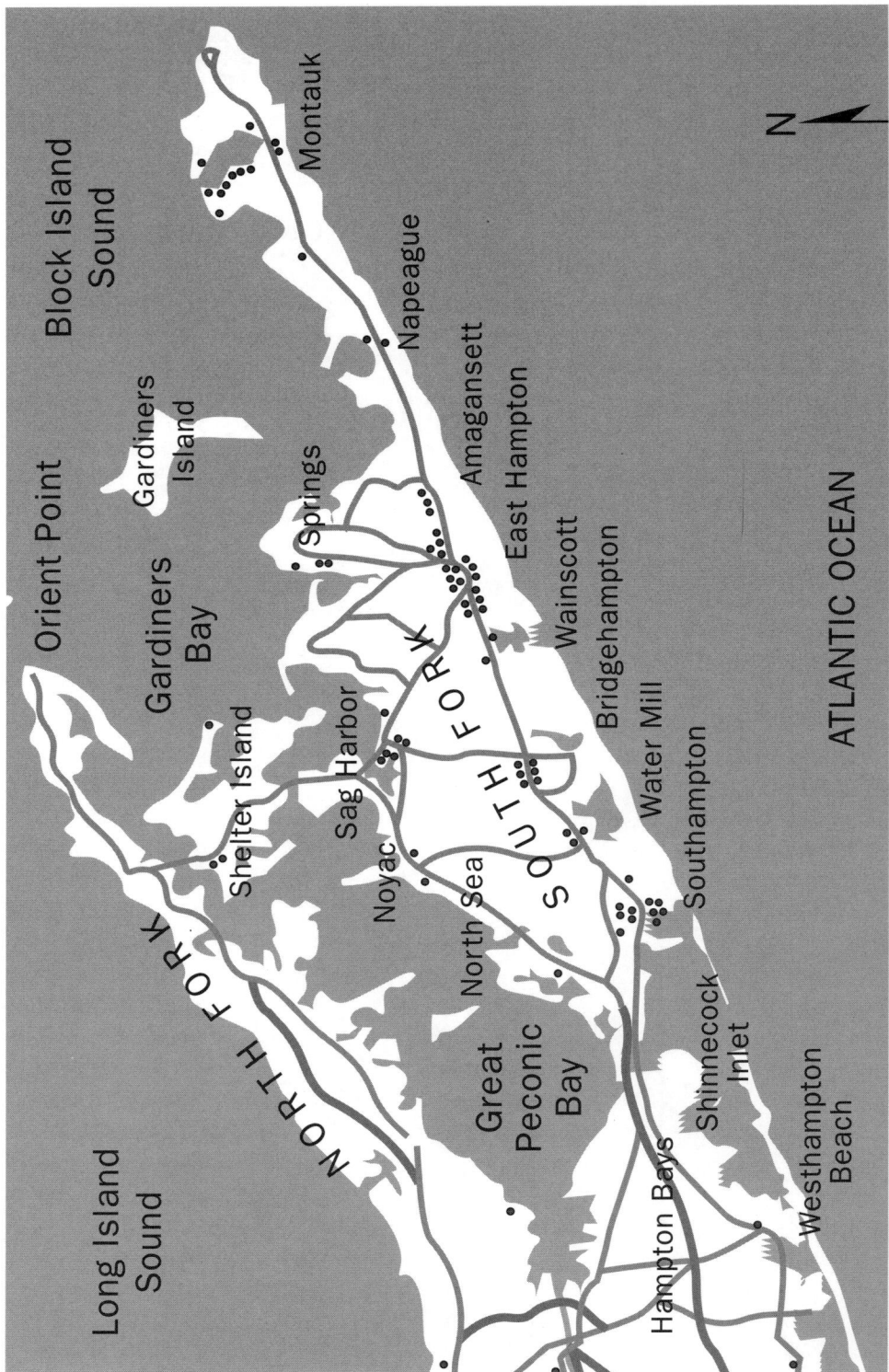